CASEY RESEARCH'S HANDBOOK FOR

# SURVIVING THE COMING FINANCIAL CRISIS

CASEY RESEARCH

# A Very Dangerous Experiment

As you read this, the biggest, most dangerous monetary experiment in history is taking place.

No one knows what the exact outcome of this experiment will be. But it's safe to say it won't be what the government expects.

How did we get here?

What can you do to protect your family from what is to come?

In regards to the first question...

In the years during and after the 2007 - 2009 credit crisis, the U.S. government engaged in a desperate attempt to stave off a global financial disaster.

Acting through the Federal Reserve, the government's defining act during this time was to drop the federal funds rate to effectively zero.

It was an extreme act...one that made it very easy for businesses, consumers, and real estate buyers to borrow money.

Americans took the Fed's lead. They borrowed trillions of dollars to fund businesses, stock purchases, commercial real estate projects, and single-family homes. They also borrowed to buy consumer items like cars, jewelry, furniture, and electronics.

By making enormous amounts of credit available, the Fed stoked the economy, stocks, and the housing market. Stocks tripled from their 2009 lows. U.S. home prices climbed from their lows. Companies with poor credit ratings borrowed record amounts of money.

In 2015, the net worth of American households reached $85 trillion, an all-time high.

On the surface, things look good. But the long period of low interest rates has created an extremely dangerous situation. By taking interest rates to zero and holding them there for five years, the Fed has created an epic amount of malinvestment and reckless speculation.

For most of the '80s and '90s, the Fed funds rate was between 5% and 10%. This relatively high cost of borrowing acted somewhat as a "brake" on funding bad business ideas, foolish real estate purchase, and "want, not need" consumer items. It didn't eliminate these things, but it did limit them.

Now, there is no brake. Just runaway borrowing and spending. The prolonged period of zero percent interest rates has completely warped the economy. We are now Alice in Wonderland.

Since borrowing is ridiculously, laughably cheap, no business idea is too dumb to fund...no $120,000 car goes unsold to someone who can't afford it...and no overpriced house sits on the market for more than a month.

The old question, *"Does it make sense to borrow this much money?"* has been replaced with *"How much can I get?"*

The U.S. government isn't the only player in this story. It's just the biggest and most powerful. The governments of Japan, China, South America, and Europe are doing the same thing. Together, central banks have created trillions of new currency units. All this new currency has flowed into assets and created enormous distortions in the global economy.

Again, we are living through the biggest, most dangerous monetary experiment in history.

Casey Research believes the funny money-fueled economy is living on borrowed time. The Alice in Wonderland economy can't last for much longer.

We've reached the point where we can't borrow any more money. Neither the interest nor the principle will be paid back. And trillions of dollars in malinvestment are about to be liquidated. It will result in a financial crisis much larger than the 2008 crisis. Not only will banks go broke, entire countries will go broke.

Like wounded animals, governments will lash out. They will act desperately to maintain power. They will pass laws that make it illegal to take money out of the country. They will freeze assets. They will raise taxes.

This brings us back to the second question we asked a moment ago...

*"What can you do to protect your family from what is to come?"*

That is the subject of this book. In the pages that follow, you'll find a complete guide for protecting your assets. These ideas are the result of years of research. They are being employed by the world's top wealth advisors. It's time you employ them as well.

Brian Hunt
CEO, Casey Research

# Table of Contents

# GETTING STARTED

If you ever wake up too early with...something on your mind, and if your uneasy thoughts extend to matters of financial survival, chances are that one of the gremlins troubling your sleep is sitting somewhere in the list just below — or perhaps it's the entire list that keeps your mind going when it should be resting.

- **The dubious dollar.** Whenever the Federal Reserve announces another round of "quantitative easing," you may hear the sound of high-speed printing presses running round the clock. They're humming away, printing still more paper dollars, and as the total grows, every new dollar is worth just a little less than the one before it. Since the financial crisis of 2008, the U.S. money supply has undergone an astounding increase, and thanks to the Fed's nonstop efforts, the supply of paper dollars is still rising rapidly. With that expansion in fiat money and with trillion-dollar federal deficits becoming the norm, it will be a miracle — and not a small one — if the dollar holds even half its value over th e next 10 years.

- **Lightning-fast asset seizures.** Government agencies have become so high-handed that today, without warning, you could be locked out of your bank account, locked out of your brokerage account, locked out of your business, and even locked out of your own home. All it takes is for one government employee to tell another that he thinks you have a giant unpaid tax bill, or that maybe you're involved in drug trafficking, or that it looks like you handle money for terrorist organizations (thousands of groups are now stuck with that label). Oh, and don't spit in that puddle: it's a protected wetland, and there are thousands of government employees who would love to protect it with your money.

When lightning strikes, there won't be a hearing, and you won't have an opportunity to defend yourself. If you're hit by an asset seizure, it will come as suddenly as a meteor crashing through your roof — and the risk of it happening is considerably greater. You'd be cut off from every ordinary source of cash and would have no means to hire a lawyer to try to recover your property.

Asset seizures are no longer rare, even though it's something most people haven't gone through. But if it does happen to you, you could be left absolutely helpless.

- **Investment controls.** From time to time, financially desperate governments impose restrictions or special taxes on owning foreign investments. The U.S. did this in small ways in the 1940s and again in the 1960s. Investment controls could look like a way to continue printing dollars without precipitating a collapse in the currency's value on foreign exchange markets. And this time, with the goal of slowing trillion-dollar outflows, the controls would need to be comprehensive and heavy-handed.

  When such controls are imposed and the padlock clicks, it becomes impractical — or even illegal — for you to buy or keep assets outside the U.S. You're barred from the opportunities for profit and for more effective diversification that can be found only in international investment markets. And without the freedom to acquire foreign currency or to spend dollars outside the US, foreign travel would be nearly impossible. You, your family, and whatever remained of your wealth would be locked inside the US.

- **Gold confiscation.** It happened to Americans in 1933, and if it happens again, there won't be any Congressional debates or other warnings. A switch will be flipped. The president will draw on his emergency powers, and you'll be compelled to sell every ounce you own at the "official" price. (The mainstream press will praise the president for his bold decisiveness.)

If that happens, the blow to investors will be far greater than in 1933. Back then, the government forced everyone to turn in his gold at the official price of $20 per ounce. Then it raised the official price to $35. In effect, the government confiscated 42% of everyone's gold. At the time of this writing, gold's official price is just $42.22 per ounce. In a mandatory turn-in at the official price, you'd lose 97% against the current market price. Gold is critical to your financial life because unlike stocks, bonds, real estate, life insurance, annuities, paper money, and your business, it doesn't depend on any formal institution — certainly not on government. The ugly irony of gold confiscation is that it would confirm your darkest worries about government at the very moment that government is stripping you of the means to be independent of it.

- **Rising income taxes.** Growing public outrage at federal deficits might lead to a period of restraint in government spending. Or it might lead to higher taxes. Or perhaps some of both. But it's not likely to lead to lower tax rates, so the odds favor your tax bill going up — if you just sit still and let it happen. Some level of income tax is tolerable for most people — and some higher level would be intolerable. Even if rates haven't yet reached the intolerable level for you, there is nothing to stop Congress from raising rates and then raising them again. During World War II, the maximum rate reached 91% (leaving just 9% for the person who earned the money). The top rate didn't recede from that level until 1963 — 18 years after the war had ended.

- **Exorbitant estate taxes and shifting rules.** The only thing politicians like more than taxing rich people is taxing dead rich people. In the last 10 years, the top rate has changed six times (with a peak of 55%), and the exempt amount has changed five times. Who knows what the numbers will be when your estate is settled? The only certainty is that paying the tax won't be a one-time experience for any family that's successful at accumulating wealth. The tax will keep grinding away at family wealth, generation after generation — unless you plan your affairs to eliminate the problem.

- **Life in a world of predatory lawsuits.** Doctors and lawyers are famously attractive targets for litigation. They're not alone. Anyone who runs a business or practices a profession lives on the lawsuit firing line. And no one is really safe. Keeping your promises, paying your bills, treating others decently, and picking up the tab for whatever mistakes you make are no longer enough to keep the litigation wolves from your door. Today, no matter how well you mind your manners, if you have substantial assets, you're a potential target for the lawsuit industry. You never know when your number might come up.

  Most people don't get sued. But anyone might. What makes the possibility so scary is that if you do get sued and lose, you could lose everything. It's a risk that no amount of liability insurance can eliminate, since an attacker can sue for your policy limit **plus** everything you own. Even if you defeat the attacker, the years of worry and the thousands you pay in legal costs mean you still lose.

- **Creative wealth confiscation.** Taxes, inflation, and currency debasement are all ways that wealth is transferred from private hands to the government. As the central planners continue their uncontrolled spending and debt accumulation, new and creative ways to expropriate wealth are being hatched that target the easy prey. Private pensions, including IRAs, are sitting ducks. The governments of Poland, Portugal, Hungary, and Argentina have all raided their citizens' private pension funds. Bank bail-ins and taxes on deposits are also on the rise. Money held in IRAs and bank accounts continues to attract the growing interest of the politicians.

These worries aren't new. People have always carried them to some degree. What is new is the now widely felt sense that such problems are imminent, waiting just around the corner.

The common thread running through the concerns is a feeling of complete exposure and vulnerability to events in your home country. If everything you have is sitting within the borders of your own country — job, business, investments, bank account, the house you live in — then you are effectively committed to going along with whatever your home government decides to do next. Whatever they come up with, if it's new taxes or regulations that hurt your income or damage your investments or that cut into your spending power, if it's restrictions on how you manage your capital, if it's a grab for retirement plan assets, or if it's an exercise of bureaucratic power aimed at you individually, you're already signed up for the whole program. You're stuck.

## Anything Goes

Such concerns aren't the work of runaway imaginations. In the US, the jaw-dropping federal deficit is real. The mountain of U.S. government debt that's accumulating in the hands of increasingly restless foreign investors is real. The extravagant, unprecedented, nonstop creation of more and more paper dollars is real. The government's increasing interference in the economy is real. The costly and dangerous U.S. involvement in foreign conflicts is real.

And those are only the symptoms. For generations, the political establishment in the U.S. has been slowly distancing itself from the idea of limited government. The central driver of today's heightened concern for financial safety is the fear that the politicians have finally detached from that principle altogether. From here on, the rule for people in power is...no rules at all. Anything goes.

So how much financial safety can you really have in such a disordered environment? The answer is that you can have a very high level of safety, but only if you go about getting it in the right way. The general approach is to move a sizeable portion of your financial life to hospitable places outside of your home county. It's not as easy as buying a BIG CAN O' SAFETY and taking it home with you. Protecting your wealth in the present environment requires some careful planning and, for most people, some new thoughts that may take a bit of getting used to.

## Simple Measures

The place to start is with the simple measures for building a personal financial base in the world outside of your home country.

**Foreign bank account.** This is the simplest one of all, but it delivers something important. It protects you from being paralyzed by a lightning asset seizure. Unlike your local bank account, your foreign bank account can't be snatched by a government employee who notices your name on a list. Reaching your foreign account would require a legal process in the foreign country, which gives you time to respond and allows you to resist. And where better to go for currency diversification than to a foreign bank? A foreign bank account is also not automatically held hostage to capital controls in your home country. Those are but a few benefits of having an offshore bank account. Read about it in Chapter 2, ***Banking Abroad***.

**Gold ownership and storage.** Gold's reliability as a store of wealth doesn't depend on the health of the U.S. or any other economy. It's the one naturally international financial asset. Even if you store it locally, owning gold ensures that you'll be able to participate in the world economy regardless of economic conditions at home. You'll be even safer if you store part of your gold in a second country — or a third or a fourth. Read about the broad menu of choices for buying and storing gold in Chapter 3, ***Gold: 24K Purchasing Power***. You don't need to use them all, but don't pick just one.

**The other stock markets.** By investing in world markets, you can reduce your dependence on events in the US. Chapter 4, ***International Stocks and Markets***, shows you how to get started.

## More Ambitious

Some of those steps may in fact seem a bit exotic to you now, but that will change once you begin to take the simplest ones. Then you'll probably be ready to do more to raise your level of financial safety.

**Teach your IRA to travel.** Your IRA may already be one of the most important elements of your financial life. There's a way to make it more secure and grow even faster: let your IRA become a citizen of the world. It doesn't need to stay crammed into a mutual fund or brokerage account in the US. It can travel. It can own rental units in New Zealand or hold gold in Austria. It can have a brokerage account in Singapore. It can even own a business renting beach umbrellas in Bimini. And whatever portion of it stays in the U.S. can be invested with much greater freedom than it has now, for much better returns than you've been getting. Plus, having your IRA offshore can help protect you in case the government makes a grab for retirement savings.

You'll find the complete story in Chapter 7, ***Give Your IRA an Accent***. And you'll learn how to build a barrier to protect your IRA from any investment restrictions that would hit ordinary IRAs.

**A warmer welcome.** Most foreign banks and brokers dread being pulled in to the U.S. regulatory net, so few will accept business from U.S. individuals. If your hope for financial safety calls for diversifying outside of the US, you know you can't do so unless there is some place for you to diversify into. Maybe no one will take your business, or if they do take it, they may later turn you out, as most Swiss banks recently have done to their U.S. customers, including customers of long standing. At many institutions, you'll get a warmer welcome if you walk in the door with a foreign face. The easiest and cheapest way to do so is to use a non-U.S. limited liability company to hold your investments. It can open an account where an American cannot. And it can be a discouraging barrier for any would-be lawsuit attacker. It also can be a big help in estate planning. To understand how you can use a foreign LLC, consult Chapter 8, ***Foreign Limited Liability Company***.

**The permanent solution.** The complete and permanent solution to every threat to your wealth is an international trust that puts your wealth in a different and much friendlier legal environment. Trust assets won't be subject to laws, regulations, asset seizures, judgment creditors, capital controls, or gold confiscations in your home country. And in the long run, the trust completely disconnects from the tax system in your home country. No, it's not simple, but it is far and away the most powerful arrangement you can have. Chapter 9, ***International Trusts***, shows you how it works.

## Still More

**A place to hang your hat.** It's a great comfort to know there's a second country you can go to without being a stranger. Finding, buying, and preparing that second residence far from home takes some effort and foresight. Chapter 5, *At Home on a Foreign Shore*, tells you how to go about the task and explains all the ancillary benefits.

**An internationalization grand slam.** In baseball, a grand slam is the most potent offensive move possible in a single play. Similarly, owning real estate in a foreign country is an internationalization grand slam, because it accomplishes so much in a single move. In Chapter 6, *Real Estate: A Global Perspective*, we show how much you can accomplish by establishing a safe haven abroad and which countries are today's best choices.

**Plant a digital flag abroad.** An easily overlooked element of internationalization is your online location. Reducing political risk to your digital life is as important as it is with reducing risk to your savings, your income, and yourself. In Chapter 11, *Diversify Your Digital Presence*, we show how to keep more of your personal and business data and your digital trail outside of the U.S. or other home jurisdiction.

**Mobility insurance.** Most of us consider the freedom to travel as a right, but governments view it as a privilege they control. Have a tax dispute with the IRS? Delinquent on a student loan? Sorry, your passport has been suspended. A second passport empowers you to avoid travel restrictions. And it may open doors to a broader selection of investment opportunities. Of course, getting a second passport means first getting a second citizenship; we lay out the different ways to go about this in Chapter 10, *A Bridge Far Enough*.

**Resources.** Ideas are just the starting point. Whatever steps you decide to take to move toward a higher level of financial safety, you'll need the specific knowledge, skills, and services of others. You'll need connections. You'll find them in Chapter 13, *Resources*, which identifies financial institutions and professionals that understand what you are trying to accomplish and are ready to offer real help.

**U.S. reporting requirements.** The rules can always change, but right now there are no limitations on the amount of money you can send out of the U.S. and no limitations on the investments you can buy. But as you might imagine, no one in the government is going to send you a letter praising your wisdom and foresight in spreading your assets internationally. Instead, largely through the IRS, the government has imposed a series of reporting requirements, every one of them backed up with the threat of serious penalties.

If you're a U.S. taxpayer, the biggest mistake you can make in internationalizing your financial life isn't walking into the wrong foreign bank or buying the wrong foreign stock. The biggest mistake would be failing to do the required reporting. To help you appreciate the scope of the reporting requirements, Chapter 12, *Foreign Account and Asset Reporting*, discusses the ones most likely to apply. Familiarity with these rules can save you considerable grief, but it probably would be a wrong turn (and certainly no fun) to try to become an expert on the topic. Instead, follow the first rule of prudence for dealing with the reporting matter: let your accountant know what you're doing.

# BANKING ABROAD

Until just a few years ago, the easiest route to international diversification was simply to open a foreign bank account. As recently as 2008, an American could get an account at a foreign bank with little more than a passport and a minimum deposit.

That was then. Today, skirmishes between foreign banks and the IRS and the growing reach of reporting regulations have made it progressively more difficult for a U.S. citizen to open a foreign bank account. But the task is still far from impossible, and the benefits to be gained make it worth the effort.

## Advantages of a Foreign Bank Account

You may wonder, "What's the difference between having an account at Bank of America and having a foreign bank account?"

The truth is, there's possibly all the difference in the world.

Here are the top reasons why you need a foreign bank account.

### Reason #1: Dilute Your Political Risk

The biggest risk you face today is not market or financial risk — as big as those risks are — but rather the risk from your own government.

There's no doubt this kind of risk is rising in most parts of the West. Governments are sinking deeper into insolvency. They're turning to the same desperate measures they always have throughout history, and that's a big threat to your savings.

It's only prudent to expect more bank deposit confiscations, retirement savings nationalizations, and capital controls, among other destructive actions.

If you think these kinds of things can't happen in your country, think again.

According to Judge Andrew Napolitano, "People who have more than $100,000 in the bank are targets for any *government* that's looking for money to shore up its own inability to manage its finances."

A big part of any strategy to reduce your political risk is to place some of your savings outside the immediate reach of the thieving bureaucrats in your home country. Obtaining a foreign bank account is a convenient way to do just that.

With a foreign bank account, your home government can't easily confiscate your savings, freeze your account, or devalue your savings with a couple of taps on the keyboard. And if your government imposes capital controls, an offshore bank account will help ensure that you can access your money when you need it the most.

Governments can impose capital controls in different ways. A government might prohibit trading currencies except at the prices it sets. It might limit the amount you can send abroad. It might require you to obtain a license to buy foreign currencies or assess taxes and fees on outbound money.

The worst case would be an outright ban on outbound transfers. Your money would be trapped inside the country.

Foreign exchange controls, if they happen, will come suddenly and without warning. The evening news hour will be interrupted with a broadcast from Washington DC, where a stern government official will announce that in order to protect our liberty and counter economic terrorism, the ability to transfer cash out of the country has been suspended, effective immediately.

It is crucial that you move a portion of your savings to a foreign bank account ahead of any such announcement. The door to foreign banking is still open, but for how long is uncertain. Having some money at a financially sound bank in a safe jurisdiction will help protect your wealth from the future actions of the U.S. government.

In short, your savings in a foreign bank will largely be safe from any madness in your home country.

## Reason #2: Sound Banking Systems and Banks

Almost all of the banking systems in Western countries are fundamentally unsound — leveraged to the hilt and backed by the promises of insolvent governments. Worse, most of these banks only keep a tiny fraction of cash on hand to meet customer withdrawal requests. This means that in the event of a financial shock like another Lehman-style event, you could have trouble accessing your money. Many U.S. banks recklessly gamble away customer deposits on risky bets like mortgage-backed securities.

The scariest irony is that public confidence in the entire banking system rests on the assurances of the FDIC — a government institution that itself will need a bailout in the next U.S. banking crisis.

If you look to bank in a jurisdiction with low debt and a history of a stability, you can find banks that don't gamble with customer deposits (i.e., your money), are much better capitalized, keep more cash on hand, and are much more conservatively run than those in the US.

The right foreign bank can be a responsible custodian of your hard-earned savings.

## Reason #3: Asset Protection

Maybe you think it's just other people who live on the lawsuit firing line... and you live somewhere else. Think again.

The Legal Resource Network reports that 15 million lawsuits are filed in the U.S. every year.

That works out to a new lawsuit for one out of every 12 adults each year... year after year. Unless you're exceptionally lucky, sooner or later your turn will come. You're not going to like it.

It's no fluke that 80% of the world's lawyers — over 1.2 million of them — work in the US. That's where the action is. Your money is the trophy they're competing for.

While there is no such thing as 100% protection, a foreign bank account can help make you a hard target.

All it takes is your name appearing on the radar of any of the dozens of bureaucratic busybody agencies, and your U.S. bank account can be frozen or seized without warning. No investigation. No jury of your peers. No presumption of innocence. The flimsiest suspicion will suffice to lock you out of your U.S. bank account.

No U.S. government agency has the power to freeze a foreign bank account. If you are ever the target of a lightning seizure or asset freeze, the cash you've secured in a foreign bank account would give you the means to fight back and also to pay your bills while you're doing it.

## Reason #4: Currency Diversification

Holding foreign currencies is a great way to diversify the risk in your portfolio, protect your purchasing power, and internationalize some of your savings.

But chances are your domestic bank offers few — if any — options to hold foreign currencies.

Foreign banks, on the other hand, commonly offer convenient online platforms for you to hold foreign currencies.

## Reason #5: Higher Interest Rates for Your Deposits

In what amounts to a war on savers, the European Central Bank and the Fed have manipulated interest rates to near historical lows. These artificially low interest rates transfer wealth from savers — who would otherwise enjoy higher returns on their deposits — to borrowers. In fact, if you live in the West, there's a good chance that the interest you're earning on your savings isn't even keeping pace with the real rate of inflation.

If you look abroad, though, you can find banks that pay interest rates significantly higher than what you'd find at home.

## Reason #6: Ensure Access to Medical Care Abroad

In the case you're denied or delayed treatment in your home country — an increasing possibility with the disastrous Obamacare — you may want to seek medical care abroad.

In a dramatic scenario, this could be the difference between life and death. Suppose that, for whatever reason, you cannot get the medical care you need in your home country and have to go abroad. That means you'll have to transfer money abroad to pay for it. But if capital controls are in effect, it could be difficult or impossible to transfer funds abroad to pay for the medical care you need.

This is where having an offshore bank account — which isn't held hostage to capital controls in your home country — can help ensure that you always have access to medical care abroad.

## Reason #7: The Ability to Act Quickly

When it comes to international diversification, it's always better to be a year early than a minute too late. Once a government has imposed capital controls or levied bank accounts, there's little you can do.

If you don't already have one, you should open a foreign bank account now — even if it's a small one. Just having one available — regardless of how much money you initially put in it — gives you the option to act quickly and transfer more money abroad if you need to. It's like having a landing spot for your money in case you ever need to use it.

## Reason #8: Peace of Mind

An offshore bank account is like an insurance policy. It helps protect you from unsound banks and banking systems and the destructive actions of a bankrupt government. It also makes you a hard target for frivolous lawsuits and allows you to pay for medical care abroad. Knowing that you have taken a strong measure to protect yourself from these things should give you a degree of mental comfort.

**Reason #9: Maximize Your Personal Freedom**

Having an offshore bank account gives you more options. More options means more freedom.

It's a crucial step in freeing yourself from absolute dependence on any one country.

Achieve that freedom and it becomes very difficult for any government to control your destiny.

**Is Having an Offshore Bank Account Legal?**

Despite what you may hear, offshore banking is completely legal and is not about tax evasion or other illegal activities. It's simply about legally diversifying your political risk by putting your money in sound, well-capitalized institutions where they're treated best.

It's no secret that it is becoming harder and harder to open an offshore bank account. Soon, it could be impossible. This is a strong incentive to get one soon — even if you don't plan to use it immediately.

Even if your home government doesn't slap on capital controls or confiscate deposits, you're no worse off for having moved your savings to a safer home. In fact, you're far better off for the reasons described above. Obtaining an offshore bank account is a prudent step that makes sense no matter what.

# Where in the World to Bank

The first step is to find a jurisdiction where you have confidence in the banking system.

Like the old adage about real estate that it is "location, location, location" that matters, so it is when you select a foreign bank: the top three considerations are jurisdiction, jurisdiction, jurisdiction.

A bank is only as stable as the legal system within which it operates, and we want a country with a history of upholding property rights, that adheres to the rule of law, and has a stable political environment, so that we can have confidence in the banking system.

There are still jurisdictions where bankers adhere to a tradition of prudence and common sense. Banks in the countries below are sound, well-regulated, and deliver professional customer service through a modern infrastructure.

You'll also want to select a bank that isn't vulnerable to U.S. pressure. A bank with zero or minimal U.S. presence means that a Washington "reach-through" into the bank's non-U.S. business will be difficult, if not impossible.

When you consider the following countries, remember that a one-and-done strategy is not adequate. Diversification applies to foreign banking, using two or more foreign banks is only prudent. There is never an absolute guarantee about the health or safety of any bank.

Ultimately, personal priorities will determine which bank has the services and location that fill your needs.

- **Switzerland.** Switzerland has earned its reputation as a premier banking center through its long history of sound and stable banking. Swiss banks are regulated by the Swiss Federal Banking Commission, whose oversight has ensured that they maintain some of the strongest balance sheets among the world's banks. Swiss accounts are also backed by several deposit insurance programs, including the basic CHF100,000 protection, which applies equally to foreign clients.

  Today, few Swiss banks welcome Americans. For the determined, expect to visit the bank in person and bring a large check — $500,000 is the minimum investment needed to begin a conversation with Swiss bankers.

  There are alternatives. For a personal account, consider using an intermediary or open an account for an international trust or foreign LLC. See "A Back Door into Foreign Banks" below.

- **Austria.** If Europe is where you want your account to be, Austria is a no-compromise alternative to its Swiss neighbor. With strict banking laws that safeguard personal information, Austria may offer greater privacy than Switzerland once did. Although limited banking information is exchanged with other governments, individual account information has bulletproof secrecy against private creditors.

  Austria also has multiple deposit insurance guarantees that include coverage for €100,000 per account (the EU-required minimum). With the exception of a bank that was nationalized in 2009, no Austrian bank has failed since 1939.

  More important, many Austrian banks will work with U.S. citizens and offer private banking services with reasonable account minimums.

- **Canada.** The country's biggest advantage as a banking location is proximity. Many banks will open accounts for Americans; just visit a branch of your chosen bank with a passport and proof of U.S. residency (a utility bill should do).

  Although outside the US, Canadian banks are not as foreign as you might like. Expect a Canadian bank to behave as a *de facto* branch of the U.S. banking system; it may acquiesce to arm-twisting by the IRS or Treasury Department. To mitigate that risk, avoid banks with a big U.S. presence (Toronto Dominion; Bank of Montreal) and favor banks such as Scotia Bank, Royal Bank of Canada, and Canadian Western Bank, which have lower profiles in the US.

  Nonetheless, Canadian banks are well-capitalized and regulated. Accounts are insured up to C$100,000 by the Canada Deposit Insurance Corporation, subject to certain limitations (see link for details).

- **Cook Islands.** This small country northeast of New Zealand (New Zealanders think of it the way Americans think of Hawaii) is entirely independent of the US. Most airline connections are through New Zealand, Australia, and Tahiti. Local financial institutions reach world markets through Hong Kong, Singapore, Switzerland, and other European jurisdictions. The Cook Islands doesn't need the US, and asset protection is one of the country's main industries.

- **Hong Kong.** Hong Kong is a major financial hub for mainland Chinese wealth, as well as an established financial center for Western companies that do business in Asia. Like those in its Asian neighbor Singapore, Hong Kong's banks are well-regulated, and the city's financial infrastructure is highly developed. Accounts (other than time deposits with maturities that exceed five years) at banks that are members of the Hong Kong Deposit Protection Scheme are guaranteed up to HK$500,000 (US$65,000).

- **Panama.** Panama has grown into one of Latin America's primary banking centers, furthered by its well-capitalized and regulated banking system and sound banking practices. Despite its advanced infrastructure, service quality may fall short of what a customer would expect from a U.S. bank.

    Panama does not have deposit insurance; if a bank goes under, depositors become creditors of the bankrupt entity. However, bank failures are rare. Because the government doesn't offer a rescue service for troubled institutions, banks are careful not to overextend their balance sheets. When there is no lifeguard, swimmers are cautious.

    Panama is easy to get to for Americans.

- **Singapore.** The culturally diverse city-state's well-capitalized banks attract capital from all parts of the world.

Singapore's banking system is well-regulated and transparent and delivers a high level of professional service. Singapore has never had a bank failure. The government's deposit insurance program guarantees accounts up to S$50,000 (roughly US$35,000). And banks offer some unusual products, including accounts tied to the price of gold and silver. Generally speaking, Singapore banks will open accounts for Americans, but a personal appearance is required to satisfy the identification protocol.

---

### Mind Your Manners

Criminal prosecutions of foreign banks by the U.S. Justice Department for assisting U.S. clients to avoid tax reporting has put foreign bankers on edge. This is one reason many foreign banks simply refuse to do business with Americans. When you deal with foreign bank personnel, it pays to behave professionally. Any hint of impropriety—whether real or imagined—can lead the bank to reject you as a customer. Questions like "Do I have to report this account to the IRS?" or "will this account help me avoid capital controls" or "How can I avoid paying tax on the interest I'll earn?" will ruin your welcome. Even though a bank may indicate that it accepts U.S. clients, no bank will accept just any U.S. client. The final determination is at the discretion of bank personnel.

You will most likely be asked something like "You live in the US...why do you want to open a bank account in Hong Kong?" A proper response would be, "I'd like to invest in Hong Kong. I also would like to own Hong Kong dollars, and I'd like to store some of my savings in the safe and stable Hong Kong banking system." A response like this will give you a good chance at a successful outcome.

---

## Make Your Move

Once a jurisdiction (or two) is selected, your next move will be to research the country's banks to determine which are financially sound. This should include a basic review of the bank's financial statements. At the top of your list should be two questions: Is the bank profitable? How much cash does it have relative to deposits (the reserve ratio)?

Don't let deposit insurance lull you into complacency about scrutinizing the health of a bank. Yes, you will get your money back. But any amount on deposit that exceeds the insured limit will be lost, and you might not be made whole.

If you go the do-it-yourself route, the Internet will be your best resource. When you contact a bank, be very clear that you are a U.S. citizen, are not a resident in its country, and would like to open an account. Indicate the amount you intend to deposit. Don't be deterred if you receive a cool reception over the phone, and be prepared to hop on a plane to seal the deal.

Before you board the shuttle to the airport, ensure that you understand exactly what documentation the bank will need to open an account.

Last, be prepared to answer questions from bank personnel about why you want to open an account at the bank. Appropriate responses include the desire to invest in the country; to diversify some of your assets into a foreign currency; to access a broader range of investments in the region; or for wealth management services offered through the bank. There are other reasons, of course, and your personal situation will shape your answer.

Do not, however, use the words "tax" or "tax shelter," or any other derivative of these in your response. Foreign bankers are already on edge about handling U.S. clients due to FATCA reporting requirements and the scrutiny of the U.S. Justice Department. The slightest hint that you seek some sort of tax advantage — even if it is completely legal — could spook the bank and cause it to deny you an account.

For the names of banks in various countries that you might consider investigating further, see Chapter 13, *Resources*.

## Back Door to Foreign Banks

There are alternate routes to a foreign bank account.

- Work with an international asset manager that will act as your intermediary to open a foreign bank account. See Chapter 13, *Resources.*

- If your preferred foreign bank doesn't accept U.S. clients, it may open an account for a foreign company even if it's owned by a U.S. person or for an international trust. More on this in Chapters 8 and 9.

- A foreign brokerage, unlike a foreign bank account, is generally much easier to open remotely. Establishing a foreign brokerage account could be a relatively easy way for you to establish a foreign financial account without having to travel.

A foreign bank account is a smart move and a simple step toward international diversification. It can add to your financial safety...but only if you satisfy the reporting requirements explained in Chapter 12. Inform your accountant of your foreign accounts. He or she will need to prepare the IRS forms and other reports to keep the accounts from turning into a problem.

— 3 —

# GOLD: 24K PURCHASING POWER

Given the runaway deficits and trillion-dollar money-printing schemes of so many of the world's governments, the need to protect the purchasing power of your capital from currency devaluation makes gold a must-own asset. Gold has served as money for centuries, and you can count on it to survive the great dying-off of paper currencies that's likely to occur in the coming years.

Gold, which is value dense and easy to transport, has always been an inherently international asset. There is nothing at all American, French, Russian, Chinese, Nigerian, Brazilian, or Australian about it. If you could take only one step toward internationalizing your financial life, buying gold would be it. The second step would be to store some of that gold in another country.

There are many ways to go about investing in gold — bars, coins, paper gold, storage programs foreign and domestic, and self-storage at home and overseas. Each of them entails advantages and disadvantages. Since none of them are the best way, it's best to use more than one — or perhaps all of them.

## Physical Bullion

The medium of gold ownership that does the most to reduce your dependence on the paper and electronic financial system is physical bullion. This means buying bars or coins.

## Gold Bars

Only bars that carry the hallmark of a well-recognized fabricator are worthy of your money. Fabricator names you're likely to encounter when you buy from a reputable dealer are:

- PAMP

- Johnson Matthey

- Engelhard

- Credit Suisse

- Heraeus

Gold bars in the sizes shown in the following table are widely available.

| Size |
| --- |
| 400 oz. |
| 100 oz. |
| 1 kilogram (32.15 oz.) |
| 10 oz. |
| 5 oz. |
| 100g (3.21 oz.) |
| 1 oz. |

Generally, the smaller the bar, the greater the premium you'll pay over the spot price of gold.

Some dealers trade each form of bullion at a quoted price plus or minus a commission (depending on whether you're buying or selling). Other dealers trade a given form of bullion at two quoted prices — a higher price if you want to buy and a lower price if you want to sell. With either pricing convention, the percentage spread between the price for buyers and the price for sellers tends to be greater for small bars than for large bars. Neither pricing convention is more advantageous to you than the other.

## Bullion Coins

A bullion coin is a coin valued primarily for the gold it contains. Like bars, bullion coins also come in various weights, but the most popular coins contain one ounce of pure gold, and most also contain a dose of copper for the sake of durability. The coins normally trade at a modest premium to the value of their bullion content, percentage premiums being greater for smaller coins[1].

The following are the most actively traded bullion coins:

| Issuer | Name | Gold Content (oz.) | Face Value |
|---|---|---|---|
| US | Eagle | 1 | US$50 |
| | | 0.5 | |
| | | 0.25 | |
| | | 0.1 | |
| US | Buffalo | 1 | US$50 |
| Canada | Maple Leaf | 1 | C$50 |
| | | 0.5 | |
| | | 0.25 | |
| | | 0.1 | |
| South Africa | Krugerrand | 1 | None |
| Austria | Philharmonic | 1 | €100 |
| Australia | Nugget | 1 | A$100 |
| China | Panda | 1 | 500 Yuan |

## Coins vs. Bullion

The effective spreads between buying and selling prices for coins is higher than for the larger bars, which is a disadvantage for coins vs. bars. The offsetting advantage for coins is that they are easy to authenticate. Any dealer (and many investors) can easily determine whether a coin is genuine. This makes resale quick and easy and makes it practical to sell

[1] Numismatics are coins that are valued more for their rarity than for their bullion content. We recommend avoiding numismatics unless you're willing to devote the time to becoming a knowledgeable collector. Investing in numismatics is as demanding as investing in real estate; you must evaluate each piece astutely before buying. We also would avoid collectibles, commemoratives, and proof coins; they sell for large premiums that you're unlikely to recoup when you sell.

to someone who isn't a dealer. A bar of gold bullion is another matter. If you've stored the bar outside of an industry-recognized depository, the dealer to which you want to sell likely will require that it be assayed, which costs money and takes time.

## Gold Storage

You may want to put away a few gold coins very privately, perhaps at home, in a place you can get to quickly. But storing large amounts of gold outside of a vault is risky. It can be stolen, and if it's stored at home, you risk attracting a dangerous visitor. Here's what to look for in any commercial arrangement for storing physical gold.

**Safe and secure.** You need a vaulting facility that is physically secure and insured. Speak with management (not a customer service rep) about the security measures in place. Ask about the insurance the facility carries and request copies of the related documents, such as "proof of insurance."

**Custodial storage vs. safe deposit box.** Leaving gold in the hands of a bank, dealer, or other custodian is convenient, since it allows you to sell at any time by sending an instruction (much as you would sell shares of stock being held for you by your broker). A safe deposit box doesn't allow that convenience; selling gold stored in a safe deposit box would require you to visit the box and remove the metal.

**Safe deposit box decision: private vs. bank.** One key benefit of gold is its independence from shocks to the financial system. Storing gold in a bank safe deposit box, even a foreign one, could compromise that advantage. You even might get locked out by the sudden declaration of a bank "holiday."

Renting a box from a bank, rather than from a private vault, could compromise the privacy advantage as well. Should anyone ever suspect that you've stored gold at a particular location, a bank is more likely than a private vault to cooperate with official requests for information, and it's likely to do so without your knowledge. A private facility probably would inform you of any sniffing and thus give you time to plan.

**Custodial alternatives: Segregated vs. pooled.** If you leave gold in custody with a bank, dealer, or any other commercial service, you can choose either segregated storage or pooled storage.

With segregated storage, specific coins or bars are identified as belonging to you and are not entangled with the holdings of other customers. With pooled storage, metal belonging to many customers is commingled, often in the form of 100-oz. or 400-oz. bars. Annual fees for segregated storage are higher than for pooled storage, but the arguably greater security of segregated storage and quicker access (as explained below) is worth the extra cost for at least part of your gold.

**Withdrawing from custodial storage.** Any custodial storage program should include a straightforward, unencumbered procedure for you to liquidate and/or take delivery of your holdings at any time. Should a pressing need arise, you want the ability to sell quickly and receive the proceeds or take delivery. Your gold won't be like an ATM, but access to it or to the sale proceeds should take days, not weeks.

Taking delivery of gold in segregated storage is a straightforward matter, since you're asking for the specific pieces of metal you own. You can either pick up the metal in person or have it shipped to you. Selling is also straightforward, since nearly every firm that stores gold also buys and sells it.

Selling pooled gold is also a simple procedure, but taking delivery is more complicated. Since what you own is unidentifiable ounces, not specific pieces of gold, taking delivery requires that those ounces be transformed into bars or coins. Depending on the custodian/dealer, you may have a range of choices for what you will receive, but the transformation won't be free. For accomplishing it, the custodian will charge a so-called "fabrication fee." Although the term suggests busy artisans hammering away in the back room, it in fact represents the premium for the type of gold you've asked for.

**Custodial decision.** Pooled storage has one big plus and a list of small negatives *vis-à-vis* segregated storage.

The negatives of pooled storage are:

1. **Possible delivery delays.** Normally you can get delivery of your pooled gold promptly upon your request. But from time to time (usually coinciding with fears of a financial crisis), the gold market becomes very busy, and there can be delays in getting delivery of the form of gold you want.

2. **Exit uncertainties.** Notice that the fabrication charge discussed above isn't set when you buy; it is set later, at the time you ask for delivery. And if, rather than taking delivery, you want to sell, you can only sell to the custodian/dealer, at the price it sets. Thus pooled storage entails the risk of getting squeezed by the custodian. If this happens at all, it happens only rarely, since a custodian that treated its customers as captives would do great damage to its reputation. But it is a reason to prefer a pooled storage program that's part of a larger business with a good name to protect.

3. **Operational risk.** If you buy pooled gold, you're relying on the dealer to keep an accurate account of each customer's share of the pool. Unless you are careless in selecting a pooled gold program, the chance that your gold will go missing is remote. But the risk isn't zero.

4. **Greater bankruptcy risk.** Gold in either segregated storage or pooled storage is legally the property of the customers. It is not the property of the custodian, so if the custodian were to become bankrupt, the gold should not be available to the custodian's creditors. However, the question of whether any particular piece of gold belongs to customers or to the custodian is a question of fact, and it takes time for a bankruptcy court to assess such facts. Thus a bankruptcy could mean a delay — perhaps a long one — in getting your gold. Any such delay is likely to be longer with pooled storage than with segregated storage. The reason for considering a pooled storage program in the face of these negatives is cost. Fees for segregated storage range from 0.4%

to 0.7% per year. Fees for pooled storage range from nil to not much more than that. The cost you can avoid is a good reason to not be scared off by risks that are remote. However, those risks are a compelling reason not to tie your fortune to any single pooled gold program.

## Foreign Storage

Gold stored outside of your home country gives you greater protection than gold stored locally. Foreign gold insulates you from the actions of any government or central bank, and it's beyond the easy reach of a lawsuit, creditors, or lightning seizures by government agencies at home. It's a shockproof medium of purchasing power that can be safely waiting for you in another country should you ever need it.

Deciding how best to own gold in a foreign country calls for revisiting the question of safe deposit box versus custodial storage. Gold left with a foreign custodian is a "foreign financial asset" and "foreign financial account," so it's reportable to the IRS, as explained in Chapter 12. Gold in a foreign safe deposit box is not reportable and thus has a privacy advantage.

As with most investment decisions, the choice between custodial storage and a safe deposit box is not a matter of either/or. You can do both. You'll find details on a number of foreign providers ready to help you in Chapter 13.

Most of the custodial storage programs are designed for metal you buy directly from the custodian. So what are your alternatives if you already have all the gold you care to own, but you've decided that you want to store some of it overseas?

One simple solution is to sell the bullion you want to relocate and repurchase it overseas. However, that would entail transaction costs and would accelerate the tax on any built-in gains. Alternatively, you could move some of the gold you already have.

## Gold Transportation Options

**Personal transport:** Personally transporting any sizeable amount of gold across a border is not advisable. The security headache alone should discourage the idea. And it is probably not a good idea to carry assets that are worth more than the combined annual salaries of the customs team you'll be dealing with.

In addition to the risks of uninsured losses from theft and misplacement, the biggest risk that you will face comes from the armed fellows wearing the government-issued costumes. Each country has different, often complex, and ill-defined regulations on importing/exporting gold bullion. It is very possible that customs agents in whatever country you are travelling through will not fully understand the regulations. They may decide to confiscate your metals and let the courts sort it out...if you are lucky.

In extreme cases, they might even detain you — simply for carrying gold.

If, in spite of this, you do plan to be your own courier, first check the customs regulations in your departure country, your destination country, and any transit country. You can boost your odds of success by taking a nonstop flight to your destination. Read about U.S. customs regulations at the website below:

http://www.cbp.gov/travel

**Hire a professional service:** There are specialized transport services that will ensure the safe and successful movement of your precious cargo. You'll find a list in Chapter 13. You could use such a service to deliver gold to one of the custodial storage programs that accepts such shipments, or you could use it to deliver the gold to you personally at a safe deposit box facility, such as one of the establishments in Austria, Singapore, Panama, or Dubai that Chapter 13 also identifies.

# Devising a Plan

Like all worthwhile endeavors, storing gold requires planning and effort, but the programs cited in Chapter 13 make it easier than you might think. The effort you invest today could pay you major dividends in the future.

As you devise your own plan, keep these guidelines in mind:

1. **Diversify among different media.** Every form of gold we've discussed is good, and none is perfect.

2. **Diversify among institutions.** Don't rely absolutely on any one bank, broker, dealer, or custodian.

3. **Diversify geographically.** Keep some of your gold in the US, close at hand, so that you can get to it as circumstances require. Keep the rest of it outside the US, ideally in countries that you visit or where you wouldn't mind spending some time.

4. **Don't get stalled trying to devise the perfect plan.** The only imperative is to get started. If you don't yet own any gold, get some now, even if it's only a single coin. If you have gold but all of it is in the US, move some now, even if you only move a little.

# — 4 —

# INTERNATIONAL STOCKS AND MARKETS

Investing in foreign stocks reduces your exposure to economic conditions in the US. Although the fluctuations in foreign markets — especially the markets of the more developed countries — tend to be strongly correlated with movements in U.S. markets, the correlation is far from absolute. So if diversification is part of your formula for dampening your portfolio's volatility, adding foreign stocks to the mix will reduce your overall level of risk and uncertainty. Or, if you're a bargain-hunting stock picker, foreign markets give you a bigger and better-stocked field in which to hunt.

## Country ETFs

By far the simplest way to diversify into markets outside the U.S. is with U.S.-listed exchange-traded funds that hold foreign stocks. For example, if you want to invest in Vietnam, you can buy shares in the Market Vectors Vietnam ETF (VNM), which holds shares in 30 Vietnamese companies. You can trade country ETFs through any U.S. stockbroker.

Below is a list of ETFs dedicated to the stocks of a particular country or region.

| Ticker | Country | Name |
| --- | --- | --- |
| ARGT | Argentina | Global X MSCI Argentina ETF |
| EWA | Australia | iShares MSCI Australia |
| EWO | Austria | iShares MSCI Austria Capped |
| EWK | Belgium | iShares MSCI Belgium Capped |
| BRF | Brazil | Market Vectors Brazil Small-Cap ETF |

| Ticker | Country | Name |
|--------|---------|------|
| EWZ | Brazil | iShares MSCI Brazil Capped |
| EWC | Canada | iShares MSCI Canada |
| ECH | Chile | iShares MSCI Chile Index Fund |
| FXI | China | iShares China Large-Cap |
| GXC | China | SPDR S&P China ETF |
| PGJ | China | PowerShares Golden Dragon China ETF |
| XPP | China | ProShares Ultra FTSE China 50 |
| GXG | Colombia | Global X MSCI Colombia ETF |
| EDEN | Denmark | iShares MSCI Denmark Capped |
| EGPT | Egypt | Market Vectors Egypt ETF |
| EWQ | France | iShares MSCI France |
| EWG | Germany | iShares MSCI Germany Index Fund |
| GREK | Greece | Global X FTSE Greece 20 ETF |
| EWH | Hong Kong | iShares MSCI Hong Kong |
| EPI | India | WisdomTree India Earnings ETF |
| INDA | India | iShares MSCI India |
| INDL | India | Direxion Daily India Bull 3x ETF |
| PIN | India | PowerShares India ETF |
| EIDO | Indonesia | iShares MSCI Indonesia |
| IDX | Indonesia | Market Vectors Indonesia ETF |
| EIRL | Ireland | iShares MSCI Ireland Capped |
| EIS | Israel | iShares MSCI Israel Cap Invest Mkt Index |
| EWI | Italy | iShares MSCI Italy Capped |
| EWJ | Japan | iShares MSCI Japan |
| EZJ | Japan | ProShares Ultra MSCI Japan |
| JPP | Japan | SPDR Russell/Nomura PRIME Japan ETF |
| EWM | Malaysia | iShares MSCI Malaysia |
| EWW | Mexico | iShares MSCI Mexico Capped |

| Ticker | Country | Name |
|--------|---------|------|
| UMX | Mexico | ProShares Ultra MSCI Mexico Capped IMI |
| EWN | Netherlands | iShares MSCI Netherlands |
| ENZL | New Zealand | iShares MSCI New Zealand Capped |
| NORW | Norway | Global X MSCI Norway ETF |
| EPU | Peru | iShares MSCI All Peru Capped |
| EPHE | Phillipines | iShares MSCI Philippines |
| EPOL | Poland | iShares MSCI Poland Capped |
| PGAL | Portugal | Global X FTSE Portugal 20 ETF |
| RBL | Russia | SPDR S&P Russia ETF |
| RSX | Russia | Market Vectors Russia ETF |
| EWS | Singapore | iShares MSCI Singapore |
| EWSS | Singapore | iShares MSCI Singapore Small-Cap |
| EZA | South Africa | iShares MSCI South Africa |
| EWY | South Korea | iShares MSCI South Korea Capped |
| EWP | Spain | iShares MSCI Spain Capped |
| EWD | Sweden | iShares MSCI Sweden |
| EWL | Switzerland | iShares MSCI Switzerland Capped |
| EWT | Taiwan | iShares MSCI Taiwan |
| THD | Thailand | iShares MSCI Thailand Capped |
| TUR | Turkey | iShares MSCI Turkey |
| EWU | UK | iShares MSCI United Kingdom |
| VNM | Vietnam | Market Vectors Vietnam ETF |

| Ticker | Region | Name |
|--------|--------|------|
| AFK | Africa | Market Vectors Africa ETF |
| GAF | Africa, Middle East | SPDR S&P Emerging Middle East & Africa ETF |
| ACWI | All World Index | iShares MSCI ACWI |
| AND | Andean Region | Global X FTSE Andean 40 ETF |

| Ticker | Region | Name |
|--------|--------|------|
| ASEA | ASEAN Countries | Global X Southeast Asia |
| BIK | BRIC | SPDR S&P BRIC 40 ETF |
| BKF | BRIC | iShares MSCI BRIC |
| VWO | Emerging Markets | Vanguard FTSE Emerging Markets ETF |
| EEM | Emerging Markets | iShares MSCI Emerging Markets |
| EFA | Europe, Australasia and Far East | iShares MSCI EAFE Index |
| EZU | European Monetary Union | iShares MSCI EMU Index |
| FRN | Frontier Markets | Guggenheim Frontier Markets ETF |
| ILF | Latin America | iShares S&P Latin America 40 |
| EPP | Pacific ex-Japan | iShares MSCI Pacific ex Japan |

# American Depositary Receipts

If you want to include a particular foreign stock in your portfolio (rather than a basket of stocks), you may be able to do so with an American depositary receipt (ADR) for the stock, which you can purchase through your U.S. broker. The process is no different than trading any other security. The table below lists the foreign stocks that are traded in the U.S. as ADRs.

| Company Name | Country | Ticker | Primary Industry |
|--------------|---------|--------|------------------|
| PetroChina Co. Ltd. | China | PTR | Integrated Oil and Gas |
| China Mobile Limited | Hong Kong | CHL | Wireless Telecom Services |
| Royal Dutch Shell plc | Netherlands | RDS.A | Integrated Oil and Gas |
| HSBC Holdings plc | United Kingdom | HSBC | Banks |
| BHP Billiton Limited | Australia | BHP | Metals and Mining |
| Toyota Motor Corporation | Japan | TM | Automobile Manufacturers |
| Novartis AG | Switzerland | NVS | Pharmaceuticals |
| Anheuser-Busch InBev | Belgium | BUD | Brewers |
| BP p.l.c. | United Kingdom | BP | Integrated Oil and Gas |

| Company Name | Country | Ticker | Primary Industry |
|---|---|---|---|
| Vodafone | United Kingdom | VOD | Wireless Telecom Services |
| Sanofi | France | SNY | Pharmaceuticals |
| Ecopetrol SA | Colombia | EC | Integrated Oil and Gas |
| Total S.A. | France | TOT | Integrated Oil and Gas |
| Unilever plc | United Kingdom | UL | Packaged Foods and Meats |
| GlaxoSmithKline plc | United Kingdom | GSK | Pharmaceuticals |
| Petrobras | Brazil | PBR | Integrated Oil and Gas |
| Rio Tinto plc | United Kingdom | RIO | Metals and Mining |
| Vale S.A. | Brazil | VALE | Steel |
| British American Tobacco plc | United Kingdom | BTI | Tobacco |
| China Petroleum & Chemical | China | SNP | Integrated Oil and Gas |
| SAP SE | Germany | SAP | Application Software |
| América Móvil S.A.B. | Mexico | AMX | Wireless Telecom Services |
| Taiwan Semiconductor | Taiwan | TSM | Semiconductors |
| Novo Nordisk A/S | Denmark | NVO | Pharmaceuticals |
| China Life Insurance Co. Ltd. | China | LFC | Life and Health Insurance |
| CNOOC Ltd. | Hong Kong | CEO | Oil and Gas |
| Westpac Banking | Australia | WBK | Banks |
| Eni SpA | Italy | E | Integrated Oil and Gas |
| Banco Santander, S.A. | Spain | SAN | Banks |
| Statoil ASA | Norway | STO | Integrated Oil and Gas |
| Mitsubishi Financial | Japan | MTU | Banks |
| Itaú Unibanco Holding | Brazil | ITUB | Banks |
| Diageo plc | United Kingdom | DEO | Distillers and Vintners |
| Honda Motor Co., Ltd. | Japan | HMC | Automobile Manufacturers |
| Banco Bradesco S.A. | Brazil | BBDO | Banks |
| Barclays PLC | United Kingdom | BCS | Banks |
| NTT DOCOMO, Inc. | Japan | DCM | Wireless Telecom Services |

| Company Name | Country | Ticker | Primary Industry |
|---|---|---|---|
| Royal Bank of Scotland | United Kingdom | RBS | Banks |
| Telefónica, S.A. | Spain | TEF | Integrated Telecom Services |
| AstraZeneca PLC | United Kingdom | AZN | Pharmaceuticals |
| Sumitomo Mitsui | Japan | SMFG | Banks |
| Mizuho Financial Group | Japan | MFG | Banks |
| Banco Bilbao | Spain | BBVA | Banks |
| Nippon Telegraph | Japan | NTT | Integrated Telecom Services |
| ABB Ltd. | Switzerland | ABB | Heavy Electrical Equipment |
| Deutsche Bank AG | Germany | DB | Diversified Capital Markets |
| China Telecom Corp. Ltd. | Hong Kong | CHA | Integrated Telecom Services |
| Baidu, Inc. | China | BIDU | Computer Services |

# U.S. Broker, Foreign Market

Some U.S. brokers will execute trades in foreign markets, which should make even more foreign stocks available to their customers. In practice, however, few U.S. brokerage firms provide such a service for individual investors on reasonable terms. And those that do generally limit you to stock exchanges in developed countries.

# Foreign Broker

To reach the whole wide world of foreign stocks, you'll need an account with one or more foreign brokers. For example, a brokerage account in Singapore or Hong Kong would give you direct access to many Asian stock markets.

As an added benefit, a foreign brokerage account gives you the same kind of protection from an asset freeze that you get with a foreign bank account. If misfortune strikes and you find yourself locked out of your U.S. accounts, you still would have liquid assets that you could draw on.

You'll find contact details for specific foreign brokers in Chapter 13.

If you wish to investigate others, begin by visiting the website of the primary stock exchange in the country that interests you. There you should find a list of exchange members. If the firm you're considering isn't on the list, you probably should move on.

While you're investigating a broker, look for indications whether the firm accepts business from the US. If you don't find an answer, send an email to the foreign broker stating that you're a U.S. investor and ask for the forms to open an account.

See Chapter 13: *Resources*, for a list and description of our suggested brokers.

# — 5 —

# AT HOME ON A FOREIGN SHORE

Investing in foreign real estate is a big step. Go about it in the right way and it's a step toward big benefits, including...

**Protection from capital controls.** When a government has financial troubles that threaten the exchange value of its currency, it may be tempted to impose capital controls. Controls can include restrictions on buying investments or anything else from foreign sources and could compel you to sell your gold, foreign currencies, and/or foreign securities to the government at artificially low "official" prices. However, due to the difficulties of administration and enforcement, capital controls seldom try to force the sale of foreign real estate.

**Discouraging litigation.** Foreign real estate is not an attractive prize for someone who is considering suing you. A successful foreclosure would require an order from a court in the jurisdiction where the property is located. Seeking such an order would require significant travel and legal expenses and years of effort and attention — which add up to a powerful deterrent for a would-be attacker.

**Protection from seizures.** Owning property in another country is perhaps the safest way to store wealth abroad; barring an act of war, it is generally impossible for the government of your home country to directly seize your foreign property. There are exceptions, however. Canada, the UK, and France have agreed with the U.S. government to cooperate in seizing property owned by U.S. citizens.

**Inflation hedge, investment potential.** Being a tangible asset, real estate serves as a store of value when currencies are being debased. Well-selected foreign property also holds the potential for rental income and capital appreciation.

**Safe house outside the USA, path to naturalization.** Owning foreign real estate would enable you to quickly settle into a new country, should you ever decide to leave your homeland — and the familiarity with the country that you gained by owning a house, apartment, or patch of land would ease the transition.

In addition, many countries offer permanent residency and a path to naturalization to foreigners who make qualifying real estate investments (in Europe, for example, this includes Portugal, Ireland, Cyprus, Latvia, Malta, and possibly Spain in the near future). Owning foreign real estate also gives you peace of mind; you know you always have a place to go should you ever want or need to. At a minimum, you'll have an enjoyable vacation home and, in a worst-case scenario, a safe haven.

**Privacy.** Foreign real estate that you own personally (not through a trust or a company) entails no reporting requirements. The IRS doesn't want to hear about it. That makes foreign real estate a clear choice if you're seeking privacy for your international wealth. Income from the property would be another matter, however. If you rent out the property or sell it at a profit, the income must be reported on your personal income tax return, along with every other dime you earn.

## Choosing the Right Country

There are a number of points to investigate in deciding where to acquire foreign real estate. Above all, you should find a place that you personally enjoy and where you're comfortable spending time, since you might want or need to live there one day. That way the investment has value to you no matter what happens to the price.

Factors to consider in evaluating a country include:

**Climate.** Weather is important. Do you prefer ski boots or flip flops? Humid or arid? Are tropical storms a concern for you? Do you want a temperate climate or four distinct seasons?

**Westernized.** Are you seeking a country that is reminiscent of "back home," with American fast-food chains and other familiar retailers? Or do you want to escape an Americanized/Westernized environment?

**Language.** Would you be lost without English? Are you willing and able to learn a foreign language to some degree of fluency? The Education First website ranks countries based on English proficiency. Its top scores go to Sweden, Denmark, the Netherlands, Finland, Norway, Belgium, Austria, Hungary, Germany, Poland, Czech Republic, Singapore, and Malaysia.

**Medical Facilities.** The state and availability of medical facilities is especially important for anyone with a chronic illness. *Patients Beyond Borders* is a website that introduces patients to safe, world-class, affordable medical care options around the world. Also worth looking into is the Joint Commission International, an accreditation agency that evaluates the quality of hospitals around the world.

**Cleanliness.** Consider the level of discomfort you would feel living near poverty or in an unhealthy environment. According to the Environmental Performance Index developed by Yale and Columbia Universities, the following were the 10 cleanest countries: Switzerland, Latvia, Norway, Luxembourg, Costa Rica, France, Austria, Italy, United Kingdom, and Sweden.

**Landscape/Geography.** Are you looking for urban amenities or a rural lifestyle with quiet surroundings? Is it important for you to be near a body of water, mountains, or the beach?

**Crime.** How secure will you feel in an area where the crime rate is higher than back home? The Legatum Institute ranks the top 10 safest countries as: Hong Kong, Iceland, Sweden, Finland, Ireland, Norway, Canada, Denmark, Taiwan, and Luxembourg.

**Cost of Living.** Your money will go a lot further in some places than in others. The Cost of Living Index maintained by Mercer (a global consulting firm) ranks cities around the world for expatriate living. Among the most expensive are: Tokyo, Moscow, Zurich, Singapore, Hong Kong, Sydney, Caracas, São Paulo, and Stockholm.

**Employment Opportunities.** Will you need to find a source of income in your new country, or do you already have one? Consider places that are business friendly. The World Bank publishes a yearly Doing Business report, and Singapore consistently ranks #1 in the Ease of Doing Business subcategory.

Taxation is also an important consideration. For more in-depth details, see the free global tax guide from the website of Ernst & Young.

**Education.** The availability and quality of education options may be a factor if you intend to continue your own schooling or if you have children.

**Connectivity.** People depend on the Internet for personal and professional reasons. The availability, reliability, and quality of a country's telecommunications is something to consider.

**Other Personal Requirements.** Do you have other personal requirements (availability of certain foods for diet restrictions, gun control status, LGBT tolerance, etc.)?

After addressing these issues, you should be able to identify one or more countries that might be a good fit.

You'll need to visit each country that interests you; there is no substitute for a "boots on the ground" experience. If you've already been to the area, visit it again for an extended period, but this time evaluate things from the perspective of a resident. This means getting out of the resort hotels and renting an apartment for at least a couple of weeks.

## Legal and Financial

Once you've settled on a strong candidate, the next step is to study the location's real estate market. You will also want to consider the legal and financial implications of purchasing real estate there.

**Welcome mat.** There are still a few countries that ban foreigners from owning real estate or that impose special restrictions. Countries that restrict foreign purchasers include Switzerland, China, and Thailand, but in many cases the restrictions amount to a handicap, not a ban.

**Taxes and fees.** What's the level of property taxes? Is rental income taxed locally? What are the local tax consequences if you sell at a profit? Do you get a U.S. tax credit for the foreign tax you pay? What are the real estate agent commissions, other legal fees, notary fees, registration fees, transfer taxes?

Here's a list of countries that do not levy property taxes:

| EUROPE | CARIBBEAN | OCEANIA |
|---|---|---|
| Croatia | Cayman Islands | Cook Islands |
| Liechtenstein | Dominica | Fiji |
| Malta | Turks and Caicos Islands | |
| Monaco | | |

| INDIAN OCEAN | MIDDLE EAST |
|---|---|
| Seychelles | Bahrain |
| Sri Lanka | Isreal |
| | Kuwait |
| | Oman |
| | Qatar |
| | Saudi Arabia |
| | United Arab Emirates |

Ireland would have been on this list, but it recently adopted a property tax. This does not bode well for investors in other EU countries that conceivably could face fiscal troubles and turn to property taxes as a solution — like Malta and Croatia.

Colombia, Costa Rica, Ecuador, and Nicaragua have property taxes, but rates are very low.

Cayman Islands is notable because most Caymanians are vehemently opposed to all forms of direct taxation and have never had it in their history. That attitude and history is a good guarantor that it will be very unlikely for a property tax to be imposed any time in the future.

**Local bank account.** You will most likely need a local bank account. This will be essential for use in paying your local expenses and receiving rent money to deposit. Owning property is usually a sufficient reason for a local bank to open an account for you.

**Legal System.** Many English-speaking countries have English-style, "common law" legal systems, while most of Europe and Latin America follow "civil law" systems. Other areas have a mixed system or one based on Sharia law. You should understand the basics of the legal system in your new country and what it means for property rights and contracts. Does the country maintain property title records?

**Mortgage availability.** Few countries have a mortgage-based real estate market similar to that in the US. In most places, if you buy, you buy with cash. In some places, this can mean paying with a bag of hundred-dollar bills. The absence of mortgage financing tends to keep prices low.

**Management availability.** It's difficult to manage a property when you're not there. Make sure there's a reputable property-management service that can handle the chores that come with property ownership (routine maintenance, taxes, bills, rent collection) when you are out of the country. This is especially important if you're considering rental property. Be aware that rental management is not the same as property management. Rental management deals with the marketing of your rental property and making sure that you maximize your rental income. Expect to pay between 20-40% of your rental income on property and rental management.

**Reliability of local contractors.** If you plan to build a home or make significant renovations to an existing property, you will have to find a local contractor. If possible, obtain references from trusted sources (such as other expats) and inspect the contractor's work firsthand.

**Real estate/rental market performance.** How has the local market performed over the past few years? Is it in a boom or a bust? There may be bargains that you can find amid the collapse of a local real estate bubble by talking directly with local banks that are looking to shed foreclosed property. What are the yields in the rental market? Are there certain months of the year when the rental market is strong or weak, or other seasonal factors to be aware of?

**The residency question.** There are benefits and costs to weigh in deciding whether to seek the status of a legal resident in a foreign country. A path to citizenship and a second passport may be one of those benefits. Tax obligations may be one of the costs.

It's not necessary, and often not even desirable, to establish official residency in the country where you'd like to spend time, because you risk getting stuck in their tax system. It's usually smarter just to leave every 90 days to renew your tourist visa and not spend more than six months per year in any one country. That way, you'll be treated as a valued tourist, who should be courted, rather than as a citizen, who can be milked like a cow.

**Unregulated is the norm.** Most real estate markets (certainly those outside North America and Europe) are unregulated. You don't get the safety nets that you do in the US. You must verify everything and never take anything on faith or someone's word alone. Your best friend in this environment will be a good lawyer.

# Find the Right Lawyer

Although it may not be strictly necessary, you'll probably benefit from the assistance of a lawyer in the country in which you're planning to purchase property, especially if it's your first time through the process. He'll help ensure that you obtain clear title to the property and comply with all the local requirements and regulations. Attorneys can also help you network and become more integrated in your new city and can introduce you to other trusted local professionals, including real estate agents and building contractors. Do not rely on an attorney recommended by the seller of the property.

Finding the right lawyer may take some research — see if there is any information available online or in local newspapers. A better way would be to find other expatriates in the country and ask them to refer a trusted lawyer whom they have personally used for a real estate transaction. Cold calling law firms and letting them know you're interested in making a local real estate investment is another way. If you have any hesitation about a firm, trust your instincts and move on.

A good lawyer and firm will speak English fluently and have experience helping foreigners navigate real estate transactions.

## Find the Right Real Estate Agent

Once you know the country and city or area where you want to make a foreign real estate investment, work with local real estate agents to get a better feel for the market. That could help you recognize a bargain when you see one.

In selecting an agent, ask detailed questions that will help you assess his knowledge of the local market, such as:

- What is the average cost per square meter for apartments/condos/homes, and how has this changed over the past couple of years?

- What are the riskiest and most overvalued/undervalued properties on the market?

- How does the local building quality compare with international standards?

- What are the rental yields for apartments/condos/homes, and do you believe the underlying demographics can sustain it?

The goal is to find a real estate agent who is well informed, objective, and has an understanding of investment value and international quality standards. Otherwise you could be wasting your time.

Be careful, though: in many foreign markets, anyone can claim to be a real estate agent. You need to do some research to select a reputable agent. Searching for information online and asking expats and foreigners for recommendations is a good start.

# Popular Destinations

The purchase of a home abroad is a very personal affair. But in the many conversations we've had with those who have accomplished it or are considering it, certain countries pop up more than others. Here is a review of some we often hear mentioned favorably.

### *Argentina*

Argentina offers a rich culture, beautiful geography, low cost of living, friendly people, and fantastic wine to complement the varied cuisine. Many Argentines are of Spanish and Italian origin, and it is said jokingly that an Argentine is an Italian who speaks Spanish and thinks he's British.

Most real estate transactions are in U.S. dollars and are settled in cash — literally. It is not uncommon to pay with a suitcase full of $100s.

Foreign buyers must obtain a tax identification number, locally known as a Clave de Identificación (CDI). To apply for a CDI, you must first receive a Certificado de Domicilio (residence certificate) from a police station. Once you have the residency certificate, the foreign real estate buyer must bring it to the Administración Federal de Ingresos Públicos. After completing the requisite forms, the CDI is issued. It is recommended that you seek the assistance of someone who is fluent in Spanish and familiar with the procedure.

There are no restrictions on foreign persons owning real estate in Argentina.

### *Australia*

While Australia is renowned for its outback and beaches, it also has highly developed cities with high standards of living, including Sydney, Perth, and Melbourne.

Australia has relatively stringent restrictions on foreign ownership of real estate.

In most cases, nonresident foreigners and temporary residents cannot buy existing buildings; they must purchase new buildings or those occupied less than a year. Temporary residents may purchase existing buildings on the condition that they sell when they leave Australia. Foreign real estate transactions for investment purposes (rental or vacation) are generally prohibited.

## Belize

In many ways, Belize is more Caribbean than Central American. Formerly known as "British Honduras," it is the only country in Central America where English is the official language. Belize is one of two Central American countries that doesn't border both the Caribbean Sea and the Pacific Ocean: Belize faces the former, El Salvador the latter.

The relatively lower prices on inland properties and ease of conducting real estate transactions has made Belize a popular destination for foreigners, particularly Americans and Canadians.

Real estate transactions are conducted in U.S. dollars, and Belize places no restrictions on the foreign ownership of real estate.

## Canada

Canada is a wealthy country, prized for its natural resources and admired for its landscapes.

Canada has relatively few restrictions on foreign ownership of property, and most of the limits relate to agricultural land. A nonresident foreigner who intends to finance a real estate purchase must make a 35% down payment and obtain the mortgage from a Canadian bank. Foreign purchasers can reside in Canada for up to six months out of the year and not be tagged a resident. This prevents getting pulled into the Canadian tax system.

## Chile

Chile extends for 3,100 miles along the west coast of South America. The country is generally more efficient, modern, and politically stable than most of its South American neighbors and has the highest income per capita in Latin America.

Chile also has attractive foreign ownership laws.

Its constitution guarantees foreign real estate owners the same private property protections as Chileans. No residency or in-country presence is required to purchase property. Chile's business-friendly environment has fostered economic growth, and investing in Chilean real estate is a way to tap in to this trend.

### Costa Rica

This small Central American country is famous for its beautiful beaches on both its Caribbean and Pacific coasts. Its political history has been more stable than that of most of its Latin American neighbors.

Ownership of property near the coast is regulated, and there are restrictions under maritime zone laws. But outside of restricted zones, foreign buyers shouldn't encounter ownership hurdles. As is customary in Latin America, most real estate transactions are conducted in U.S. dollars. It is difficult to obtain financing in Costa Rica, so be prepared to secure financing elsewhere or pay cash.

### Ecuador

The level of real estate prices (and the cost of living in general) in Ecuador is among the lowest in the world, which makes the country popular with retirees on a budget. There are no restrictions on foreigners owning property.

The weather is pleasant year-round: warm on the coasts and cool in the mountains. And with cosmopolitan cities like Quito and Cuenca, Ecuador makes sense for many from a lifestyle perspective.

### Mexico

Outside of restricted zones, foreigners have the same right to purchase property as citizens. The restricted zones include areas within 50 kilometers of the coast and 100 kilometers of an international border. To purchase property in these zones, a foreigner must use a structure known as a Fideicomiso, or Mexico Land Trust.

## New Zealand

New Zealand is blessed with abundant natural beauty — mountains, rivers, lakes, plains, and beaches. The country consists of two main islands and many smaller islands. It is remote, and many areas outside the main cities are sparsely populated.

Nonresident foreigners can purchase real estate without restriction and do so without visiting the country.

The purchase of land, however, is regulated. Areas designated as "sensitive land" require permission from the government and include farms and coastal properties. Obtaining permission to buy areas of sensitive land means demonstrating that the purchase will impart economic benefits to the country.

## Singapore

This island city-state in Southeast Asia was founded by the British as a trading colony and today is one of the world's most prosperous countries. Its culture is a product of Chinese, Indian, and Malay influences.

Foreign ownership of residential property is regulated under the Residential Property Act. The act restricts nonresident foreigners to the purchase of residential units in approved developments; foreigners generally are not allowed to own detached residential property or an entire residential complex.

However, there are no restrictions on foreign ownership of commercial or industrial real estate, so long as the property is kept in use.

## Saint Kitts & Nevis

The Caribbean nation is another popular destination for foreigners to purchase real estate. Besides being a tropical paradise, the country will throw in permanent citizenship and a passport for approved real estate purchases of at least US$400,000. See Chapter 10 for more details on the St. Kitts & Nevis economic citizenship program.

## *Switzerland*

Switzerland is a wealthy and stable country famous for its strong traditions of independence and neutrality. It is not a member of the EU and only became a member of the UN in 2002.

It has long been an attractive place for foreigners to buy real estate, even though it has relatively strict limitations on the foreign ownership of property.

Nonresident foreigners are limited to the purchase of one property that must be used as a vacation home or secondary residence. A property purchase with the intent to earn rental income is not permitted (though short-term rentals are allowed).

The Swiss government allots annual quotas on the number and type of properties available for purchase by nonresident foreigners. The government of the respective canton (similar to a U.S. state) must approve the transaction; each canton has its own requirements and restrictions that can include limits on the size and location of the property and the length of time before you can sell. Swiss residents and nonresident foreigners who hold EU passports have fewer mountains to climb.

# — 6 —

# REAL ESTATE: A GLOBAL PERSPECTIVE

Any topic that includes the word "global" poses a particular challenge: where in the world to begin. As most of you reading this are likely doing so from somewhere in the Occidental part of the world, let's begin with a brief discussion of my four reasons why North American and European property is now a bad bet. Then we'll take a look at the tremendous opportunities that still remain for property investments outside of those markets.

Let's start with the premise that real estate in many markets is headed for big trouble. This is likely to be true for several reasons:

**Debt.** In the US, Canada, Australia, New Zealand, and some countries in Europe (especially the UK and Spain), property prices float on a sea of debt. During the long boom that started in the early '80s, people borrowed as much as possible to buy property. They liked the leverage to profits it gave them in a rising market. They liked the higher standard of living that borrowed money can offer. Governments encouraged homeownership in the understandable belief it would result in a more stable society, where everyone had a stake in property. Debt was a very good thing for early adopters, especially since interest rates fell — worldwide — for over a generation.

As with all markets, things became overdone. Debt grew from a manageable convenience to a necessity in buying simply because borrowed money had driven prices so high. And now, with interest rates at generational lows — and highly negative in real terms — we can absolutely count on them rising. Positive interest rates are essential if people are ever going to start saving again — which is to say, producing more than they consume and setting aside the difference. I expect interest rates to go back to at least the levels we saw in the early '80s:

12-18%. If you think the property market is bad now with all-time low nominal and real rates, wait 'till rates go to nominal and real all-time highs in this cycle, which I fully expect. Far from making society more stable, government sponsorship of unqualified homeownership will result in a huge number of bankruptcies and homeless people...a very explosive sociological problem.

The debt burden on real estate in most developed countries alone guarantees that the current bear market will be deep. The fact that governments are actively trying to prop up the markets, especially in the US, as evidenced by the Fannie/Freddie bailouts and numerous state and federal actions intended to "help" homeowners who actually can't afford to live in their current digs, only guarantees that the bear market will drag on for years longer than necessary.

**Taxes.** Property taxes are a surprisingly underrated factor when the direction of real estate is considered. These taxes vary greatly both in percentage assessment and how they're computed. But my suspicion is that throughout most of the English-speaking world, they average 1% of market value annually. In several places I can think of in the U.S. and Canada, they amount to 2%. What it boils down to is that many middle-class homeowners are paying $10-20,000 annually to the government to live in their own house. This is a significant nut to crack before every other expense. And if the tax bill isn't paid, the "homeowner" will soon find out who really owns his home.

Predictably, most local governments are heavily in debt and running deficits. As tax revenues from all sources decline, these governments will be even more squeezed for money — and at the very time their constituents are likely to be asking for more services. It's hard to say how they're going to make up the shortfall, but especially in today's "eat the rich" environment, higher property taxes are a possibility, if only because real estate is a form of wealth that simply can't be hidden.

Here's a prediction: the U.S. and Canada are two of relatively few countries in the West today that don't have an annual national wealth tax — an annual tax on net worth. Governments are increasingly going to a wealth tax for a number of reasons. It hits the rich, which is always popular with *hoi polloi,* and it gives the government an accurate baseline for each individual's wealth, which makes assessing annual income taxes that much more convenient for them. With the U.S. federal deficit recently running at a trillion dollars annually, a wealth tax is increasingly probable. Real estate is its single largest target.

People seem to have forgotten that in the 1930s and '40s, there were many thousands of tax sales of property. I think it's likely to happen again.

**Maintenance, Utilities, and Depreciation.** During the boom, maintenance and utilities were almost always overlooked as a cost of ownership. Rapidly rising prices obviated these costs. And "fixer-uppers" were viewed as opportunities, not liabilities.

Roofs need repair. Plumbers and electricians are necessary and notoriously expensive. Carpets wear out. Windows and appliances need replacement. It's not possible to live in a house without electricity, gas, heating oil, and water. These "after tax" expenses come off the top of a homeowner's income as surely as food expenses, and they're almost certainly heading up faster than the general cost of living.

The boom in housing prices caused by currency inflation and debt has diverted attention from an essential fact: houses are not investments. They are expensive consumer goods, much the way cars are. In normal times, they don't appreciate: they depreciate — certainly in real terms.

**Location, Location, Location.** Everything else being equal, these are the three most important things about real estate. Unfortunately, during the long boom, a lot of housing was built in locations that can only be described as "uneconomic." The housing was built on land that was cheap because it was far away from existing places of business and jobs. To keep costs down in an artificially booming market, "bedroom communities" arose that depended on the automobile. But with gasoline prices high and likely headed higher, the residents of those communities are finding a half-hour — or sometimes an hour or even a two-hour — commute is unaffordable, especially in the pickups and SUVs that tend to be favored by the people who live in faraway developments. And the situation will only be exacerbated by a rapidly contracting job market. I expect this factor will put substantial additional pressure on certain areas of the market, perversely exactly those where the people can least afford the strain.

It's important to look at these factors from a long-term perspective. Although they'll all sort themselves out eventually, I suspect we're talking about years, perhaps a decade, or even a generation. I recognize that implies a far worse market than most people anticipate. But the long boom was unique, and it will take a necessarily long time to sort out the distortions and misallocations of capital that were cranked into the system over 30 years.

As a consequence, with the exception of special situations, I simply can't see investing in real estate in the US, Canada, or most of the rest of the developed world, for a considerable time. While it's certainly not optimal — that ship sailed years ago — now is still a good time to sell. If you can. Should you decide to make a purchase in these countries, view it strictly as a consumer good; they're likely to be terrible investments.

But real estate is such a major asset class and it's so convenient to own property from a lifestyle point of view that the thought of not owning property somewhere and being strictly a renter understandably won't appeal to most readers. My solution is to look abroad. Which brings me to my four reasons you should seriously consider taking action. Do not view this as an academic discussion.

## Going Global

**Attitude.** As the Jimmy Buffett song says, "Changes in latitude, changes in attitude." My personal experience has always been that I (Doug Casey) have regretted things I haven't done much more than things that I have — and I've done quite a lot. But the path not taken, the door unopened, might lead to a whole new universe. Most people even today, even in North America, still have the mindset of a medieval serf. The medieval serf would typically never in his whole lifetime venture more than 10 miles from his hut, and probably not even that far. The logistics of finding something to eat and a place to sleep were simply too formidable.

Of course, today's technology has made it possible for people to drive or fly almost anywhere. But few leave their native country, perhaps out of an atavistic fear that "there might be dragons."

Living in a different culture and gaining some familiarity with a different language is one of the experiences that make life worth living. Often, transplanting the capital, experiences, and connections you have as a member of a rich society — where they're quite ordinary — can make you a big fish in a somewhat smaller pond. Think about it. Would you prefer to remain a peasant in a mud hut or take a shot at playing Marco Polo?

**Foreign Exchange Controls.** The likely imposition of currency controls in the near future will subtly put most citizens in exactly the position of a serf. One reason serfs stayed serfs is that they had no assets they could take elsewhere; that cemented them to one place. Especially since the passage of the Bank Secrecy Act of 1970, there have been more and more restrictions and reporting requirements for Americans when it comes to having assets abroad. At this point, you may still privately own stocks and bonds outside the US, as long as they aren't in a brokerage account of any type; if they are, they become reportable. Assuming that you can even find a firm willing to open an account for you...

Two important things you can still own outside of the U.S. without having to report them are a safe deposit box and real estate. I urge you to acquire both while it's still possible. It may not be possible in a year or two, because I expect some form of currency controls. These are partly because of the trillions of dollars now held outside of the U.S. (increasing by perhaps a trillion annually), which are like a ticking bomb waiting to vaporize the value of the dollar. One recent straw in the wind was the imposition of significant tax penalties on any American who renounces his citizenship.

It's impossible to say what form capital controls may take. But I think you can plan your life around the fact that the government is much more likely to control its subjects than control itself. So the prospect of their letting Americans continue sending significant capital abroad without approvals, and perhaps taxes, is becoming slim.

The nice thing about a box full of gold coins in a well-chosen country is that it's a truly private asset that's likely to appreciate substantially in the next few years. And the same is true for a nice piece of property — in addition to the fact that you can vacation on it or perhaps even use it for retirement. But again, I suspect time to efficiently acquire these assets abroad is getting short.

**Diversification.** Everybody understands the importance of diversification among investments. Accidents happen, and you don't want all your eggs in one basket. But almost everybody overlooks political diversification, which is far more important, because the political risks to your portfolio are actually greater than the market risks. Just think of the histories of some of the countries I discuss below and it will be immediately apparent. But you may be thinking: "Sure, but this is the U.S. (or Canada). We're different." Well, that's largely been true. Just as it was largely true in most countries — before it became untrue.

In years past, there was always a significant advantage to being an International Man, both from the aspect of personal freedom and financial opportunity. Today, however, that diversification is critical, simply because the U.S. has been accelerating its progress in the wrong direction. I'm not saying you need think like a Jew in Germany in the '30s, or an Eastern European in the late '40s, or a Cuban in the '50s, a Vietnamese in the '60s, a Chilean in the '70s, an Iranian in the '80s, a Bosnian in the '90s, or about a hundred other groups in various places in recent history. I'm just saying we should all realize we're part of history, and untoward things happen absolutely everywhere eventually.

**Value.** A good investor is always comparing price with value, looking for anomalies. Most real estate investors are locally oriented. That's understandable, in that they can become experts in the local market. But it necessarily limits the number of deals they can look at. And staying local limits your perceptions of value. I'd rather treat the world as my oyster in this regard. Peasant serfs tend to stay serfs if they never look beyond the next valley.

Over the last 30 years, I've basically been paid to live in certain parts of the world because the appreciation of the property I've bought there exceeded its equivalent in the US, not even counting the vastly lower cost of living. Most countries I've chosen in the past are no longer suitable; they've appreciated beyond the range of being good investments. But the world property market is always in flux. Some places today are at least as attractive as opportunities you might wish you'd taken advantage of 10 or 20 years ago. The market always presents new opportunities.

## A Quick Trip around the World

That said, let's look at some specifics — past, present, and future. In the context of the future, I'll pinpoint the best places in the world to put your real estate dollars — while you're still able to and while they're still worth something. I'm skating rapidly over the surface here.

First, a few geographical observations, and then a look at the three types of situations that always get my attention — especially when two or three characteristics are present at once.

**Europe.** Europe is even further down the slippery slope than North America. In a couple of generations, Europeans will mostly serve as maids and houseboys for the Chinese, and the European landmass will be mostly a full-scale Disneyland for Asian tourists. In the meantime, it's the front line in the ongoing War against Islam. Demographic projections show that some countries, like the Netherlands and France, will be nearly half Islamic in two generations.

Frankly, the colors of the map on the wall have been running since Day One, so I really don't care who winds up living in Europe. What concerns me is the turmoil that's likely to occur along the way.

As an investment, property in Europe is a short. Declining population, incipient culture war, overtaxed, and vastly overpriced, I just can't see it. European property as an investment makes no sense.

Yes, the UK was a fantastic deal in 1986, when the pound was at parity with the dollar. Spain was a great deal when I was writing about it at that time; property on the Costa del Sol has gone up at least six to eight times. My rationale back then was that with Spain joining the EU, masses of

Northern Europeans would move there because the weather was vastly superior and the cost of living much lower. That's exactly what happened.

**The Islamic World.** This area isn't one that most readers would consider. In the past few years, I've looked at a number of countries. I wouldn't consider any of them, but for different reasons. As for Dubai, there is no place on the planet with so much purely speculative building and so many totally empty buildings that serve no purpose other than to be sold to a greater fool. As much as I like the place, it's a gigantic accident waiting to happen. The good news is that it may present a once-in-a-lifetime opportunity after it comes unglued.

**Africa.** Africa is a fantastic place for speculators and adept entrepreneurs. But it's not a good place for a white man to try to plant roots. Racism is endemic on the continent that complains most about it. Sure, there are special situations, like Botswana, Mozambique, and Namibia — all very different, and all attractive for different reasons. But the continent is no place for the speculator who isn't on the spot to manage his property. And its political problems, which basically boil down to the government serving no purpose except to facilitate theft for those who control it, are unlikely to go away for a long, long time. Why? Because when the Europeans divided up the continent into arbitrary countries, they paid zero attention to the ethnic groups living there. Africa is going nowhere until the lines are totally redrawn. Or perhaps after the Chinese re-colonize it.

**The Orient.** China is on everyone's mind. Its progress and success are very real, and this will indeed be the Chinese century. But that doesn't mean they aren't very late in a long business cycle, much of it driven by currency debasement that's cranked huge distortions and misallocations of capital into China's economy. I expect it's going to have severe problems from several angles.

If you want to put money in the Orient — which makes sense — do it in Thailand, which will continue to draw capital from all over the world. My choice of cities is Phuket; you won't get hurt buying there. Burma is discussed below. If you're looking for an outlier with real potential and low prices that nobody ever thinks of, go to Laos. Singapore isn't cheap, but it's going in the right direction, and that seems unlikely to change. If you want a crib in a city, it's my first choice.

## Global Real Estate by Category

**Conflict Zones.** The original Baron Rothschild is famous for having said, "Buy when blood is running in the streets." The theory is eminently sound but very scary and usually logistically inconvenient to put into practice at the moment of truth.

*Zimbabwe.* Early in my writing career, I described a fantastic castle, the Leopard Rock, being run as a hotel in the mountains of Zimbabwe on the Mozambique border. I contemplated buying the place in 1979 for the asking price of $85,000 but passed because it would have been a tough lifestyle choice. Ten years later and the war over, it changed hands for $13 million. I don't know what the asking price on it might be today. With the draconian capital controls now in place in Zimbabwe, the owners would be fools to sell, at least if all the money were paid within the country. I'll bet $500,000 offshore would take it away, about the same real price as it went for 30 years ago. If you buy it or something like it in the country, you'll look like a genius when Mugabe dies.

*Burma.* In the last decade, beachfront in Thailand has probably risen 1,000%. Although it's no longer the spectacular value it once was, it's undoubtedly going higher simply because Thailand will be the prime beneficiary of tourism and investment diversification from China. But I say that only as an introduction to Burma. It's larger than Thailand and has a much smaller population, but is just as pretty and interesting. The problem, of course, is its insane government. But the generals are on their way out; it's just a matter of time. The country has a couple thousand miles of beaches, all owned by the state. I have no doubt a deal could be cut, maybe even trading free land for development. Somebody who wants to spend time in the country might make a billion dollars over the next decade as the country restructures.

*Nicaragua.* Nicaragua used to be known as a place where Contras battled Sandinistas; Reagan scared naïve Americans by implying that invaders were only a day's drive from Texas. Shortly after the civil war ended, some friends and I bought 1,500 acres with about 4 kilometers of beachfront quite cheaply. We later sold the first beachfront lots for $17,500. Those same lots are now trading at 10 times that price, and the project has become a nice community. Nicaragua is still the cheapest place in Central America, but the circumstances that induced me to use it as an example of a "conflict" country have obviously disappeared.

*Chile.* Chile was being turned into a people's republic by Salvador Allende when he was assisted in shedding this mortal coil in 1973. In 1980, I visited a man at his house in Santiago, a really splendid place that would easily sell for a few million dollars today. He allowed that in 1972, he would have sold it for $25,000, and his neighbors would have done the same. They were afraid Chile was going the way of Cuba. Chile is today the most prosperous country in Latin America and probably one of the most stable in the world. In fact, the average Chilean now has a higher net worth than the average American because of its privatized Social Security program. It's shocking how quickly things can change.

*Cuba.* Of course, on the other hand, a speculator might have actually bought in Cuba in 1959 and lost everything. But one Chile can make up for 20 Cubas. And even in Cuba, he wouldn't likely have lost everything. About half the land on that island is still privately owned, although it obviously never trades. At some point in the not-too-distant future, confiscated land and houses will likely be returned to their historic owners, as was the case in Eastern Europe in the '90s. I've been down there four times over the years and have yet to find a way that makes sense for capitalizing on the inevitable boom when the Castro brothers are replaced. But it's on the watch list.

**Cheap countries.** Buying in a war zone or a conflict country obviously taps deep value and also significant risk. But sometimes a country becomes severely undervalued because of domestic government policies, or the state of the commodity markets, or simple anomalies. Spain was an example in the '80s. So was Hong Kong, which I also wrote a lot about in that context in earlier days. Canada has been cyclically cheap several times over the past few decades, usually when prices of natural resources were down; it's no bargain today.

Argentina is likely the place to be for the indefinite future, as odd as that may sound to current-affairs junkies. Sure, it has had incredibly stupid governments. But the country's climate, location, ethnic makeup, stability (no, that's not a misprint), sophistication, culture, and extremely low cost of living are unique. There's a good chance that wealthy Europeans (who are piling into the country), plus a change in economic policy, will make the place genuinely prosperous again.

**Path-of-growth countries.** North American property investors are familiar with investing in the path of development. But it doesn't just work within countries; it works for the countries themselves.

Spain, described above, was one example. Vancouver, BC, was another, as hundreds of thousands of wealthy Orientals moved there, at first just to get a Canadian passport and have a foreign bolt-hole. And then many stayed because it may be the nicest city in North America.

Panama has been booming, and that will continue to be attractive because Panama City will become the new Miami. Uruguay is a place people don't think of in terms of growth. It's much more provincial than Argentina, which is just across the La Plata River, and considerably more expensive...but with some unique attributes.

## Conclusion

There's much, much more I can say about all these places and many others. You can't help learning a few things in the course of visiting 145 countries and living in 12.

But the purpose of this chapter is to try to get you to do something... for any and/or all of the reasons I give, in at least one of the places I've mentioned.

And do it now. Time is short.

# GIVE YOUR IRA AN ACCENT

Your IRA may be the best thing that has ever happened to your financial life. And if you're handling your IRA the way most people do, the best thing you have now could become a lot better.

To qualify as an IRA and to achieve the tax-free compounding that's at the heart of an IRA's wealth-building power, the investments in the account must be held by a licensed custodian in the US. Despite this requirement, it still is possible for your IRA to keep one foot outside the US. The arrangement that enables your retirement account to do so brings with it an advantage so great that it may make you want to hug your IRA.

## The Arrangement

Most IRA programs are sponsored by a financial institution such as a bank, brokerage firm, or mutual fund family that has something to sell. The sponsor selects a custodian and determines what investment choices — its stuff — will be available. So unless an investment is on the list of what the sponsor is selling, it's not going to get in to the IRA.

An alternative that some investors have turned to is the so-called "self-directed IRA." There is no sponsor — just the custodian and the investor. When the investor identifies an investment for his IRA, he instructs the custodian to buy it. Self-directed IRAs are used most commonly for investing in real estate, but they can go much further than that. Except for asset types found on the government's short list of prohibited investments, a self-directed IRA can invest in almost anything, including private placements, mortgages, tax liens, and equipment (for leasing).

The investment freedom that comes with a self-directed IRA can mean much better returns and faster growth, because you will, of course, gravitate toward the investments you understand best. And the returns on some investments, such as tax liens and equipment, are high because of the skill, time, and effort they require. If you're willing to do the work, the rewards will build up, tax-free, inside your IRA.

Sounds good. But there are disadvantages that come with most self-directed IRA programs, and they can be summed up in one word: cumbersome. Every transaction involves communication with and action by the custodian. That means delays, which can mean missed opportunities, and it probably means high expenses, since the custodian will charge another fee every time it lifts a finger.

A special type of self-directed IRA, an "Open Opportunity IRA," eliminates those disadvantages. The custodian directly holds just one asset for the IRA: a limited liability company that the IRA owner manages. With the Open Opportunity structure, you only deal with the custodian when you make a contribution or a withdrawal. Otherwise, the custodian is out of the picture. All the investment activity happens inside the LLC, where you're running the show on your own; the custodian isn't involved.

As Manager of your IRA's LLC, you can make the investment program as international as you want. You can open a foreign bank account for the LLC and invest in currencies. You can buy farmland in New Zealand or Uruguay. You can buy American Eagle gold coins and store them in a safe deposit box in Austria. So long as you stay away from the short list of prohibited investments and avoid self-dealing (see the box), the entire world can be your IRA's investment oyster.

## TWO BIG DON'TS

An IRA is prohibited from buying certain types of investments and from doing business with related parties.

### Prohibited Investments

An IRA may not invest in life insurance, in the stock of an S corporation, or in "collectibles." Collectibles for the purpose of this rule include art works, rugs and antiques, metals and gems, stamps and coins, and alcoholic beverages.

There is an exception for bullion coins issued by the U.S. Treasury. Under the exception, it is permissible for your IRA to buy U.S. gold, silver, or platinum Eagle coins.

### Prohibited Parties

An IRA is prohibited from engaging in almost any transaction with a "related party." Related parties include the IRA's owner and the owner's spouse, parents and grandparents, and the owner's children and grandchildren and their spouses. A trust or company is a related party if it is owned 50% or more by related parties. But an IRA owner's brothers, sisters, cousins, friends, and business partners are not related parties.

You can take internationalization even further. Your IRA's LLC can own a foreign LLC that you also manage. That foreign LLC would improve your access to non-U.S. investments.

## Roth Implications

A Roth IRA compounds investment returns without current tax, just as a traditional IRA does. The additional big benefit of a Roth is that withdrawals can be tax-free[2]. If you want that benefit, you have the option of moving all or any portion of the assets of your traditional IRA into a Roth IRA (a "Roth conversion"). But there's a cost to the conversion: except to the extent of any non-deducted contributions you may have made over the years, the value of the assets moving into the Roth is taxable income. That could mean a jumbo tax bill in the year of the conversion.

If you have assets outside of your IRA that you could tap to pay the current-year tax bill, the argument for making the conversion to a Roth is strong, despite the pain of writing a big check to the IRS. Here's the argument. While you may think of your traditional IRA as exclusively yours, in fact the government effectively owns a share of it, since no matter how the investments perform and no matter how long you wait to withdraw the money, the government will get a certain percentage.

After a Roth conversion, however, you really do own the whole thing; thus a Roth conversion amounts to a buyout of the government's share. The buyout is a very good step; its net effect (after allowing for the immediate tax cost) is to remove a chunk of your capital from the high-tax neighborhood of direct ownership and relocate it in the tax-free neighborhood of the Roth. And that is moving uptown.

With the Open Opportunity structure, the advantage of converting to a Roth can be even greater, since you can cut the tax cost of making the conversion by one-third or so.

What attracts tax at the time of a conversion is the "fair market value" of the property moving to the Roth. An asset's fair market value, as that term is used in the tax rules, doesn't refer to the asset's value to you. It refers to the asset's value to a hypothetical stranger.

With appropriate provisions in the LLC's operating agreement, the fair market value of a 50% or smaller interest in the LLC will be less than its *pro rata* share of the value of the underlying investments. The fair market value will be less — perhaps one-third less — because such a

---

[2] Beginning with the year in which you reach age 59 1/2, withdrawals from a Roth IRA are tax-free, provided that the Roth is at least five calendar years old.

non-controlling interest has no power to compel distributions from the LLC or to control it in any other way, and because it would be virtually impossible to find a buyer for the non-controlling interest without discounting the price heavily.

To benefit from such valuation discounts and save one-third or so on the tax cost of a Roth conversion, move 50% of the traditional IRA's LLC into a Roth this year. Move the other 50% next year. The total income recognized on the two transactions can be reduced to only be about two-thirds of the value of the underlying investments.

# — 8 —

# FOREIGN LIMITED LIABILITY COMPANIES

The limited liability company was invented by the Wyoming state legislature in 1971. Since then, certain countries and all of the other 49 U.S. states have enacted laws that authorize and recognize LLCs.

An LLC organized outside your home country can be a serious barrier to anyone trying to collect a lawsuit judgment against you. In addition, for U.S. investors, a foreign LLC can be the calling card that opens the door to international banks, brokerage firms, and insurance companies that would be shy about dealing with you directly, and it also can be a useful tool for limiting gift and estate taxes.

## LLC Basics

A limited liability company combines the most advantageous features of a corporation with the simplicity and (for U.S. owners) the tax efficiency of a partnership or sole proprietorship. An LLC comes into existence when you or a service you hire files a simple document with the appropriate government office in the state or country you've chosen.

An LLC's owners are commonly referred to as the "Members" of the company. The Members needn't be individuals. Trusts and other companies can be Members.

There is no limit to the number of Members an LLC may have, and most jurisdictions will allow an LLC to have just one Member (which would own the entire company). Thus you could be the sole member of an LLC, or alternatively, you and other family members or family trusts could also own interests in the company.

An LLC does not have directors. Instead, it can be managed by its

Members in town-hall fashion, or by one or more Managers. Any person agreed upon by the Members can be a Manager, even if that person is not one of the Members. Thus it is possible to completely divorce ownership from management, as would be the case if you were the sole Manager of an LLC and your family trust were the sole Member.

Neither the Manager of an LLC nor any Member is personally liable for the company's debts. This would protect you as Manager and you as Member from responsibility for any obligations the LLC might take on.

The relationship among the Members and the Managers is usually set out in a written "Operating Agreement," which is analogous to a corporation's bylaws. The Operating Agreement explains the powers and duties of the Managers and the power that the Members retain to replace the Managers. The laws in most jurisdictions place little restriction on the arrangements that Members and Managers of an LLC are permitted to agree to, although a few jurisdictions do.

A foreign LLC is cheaper to operate than a foreign corporation, since it involves no costs for directors or other management persons in the country where it is formed. And it's easier to run, since it doesn't need to observe all the record-keeping formalities of a corporation. In short, an LLC eats less and is lighter on its feet.

## Asset Protection

A creditor (such as the winner of a lawsuit against you) might hope to reach the assets of your LLC by either of two routes. First, he might ask a court to force the LLC to liquidate, in which case the assets would come back to you personally and be available to your creditors. Second, he might ask a court to foreclose on your membership interest and assign it to him.

An LLC's Operating Agreement can choke both of those routes. The Agreement can require the consent of a supermajority of the Members, or even unanimity, to liquidate the company. And it can restrict the transferability of membership interests, perhaps by requiring the approval of all the Members and/or of the Manager. But those provisions will be effective for asset protection purposes only if the court you're dealing with will respect the terms of the Operating Agreement.

In some jurisdictions, the local statutes require a court to do exactly that, so the courts will decline to touch an LLC for the benefit of a Member's creditor. In other jurisdictions, the courts will respect the terms of an LLC Operating Agreement in the face of a Member's creditor if there is some third party who would be injured by disturbing the LLC. The ideal third party is another Member. So if asset protection is one of your purposes for an LLC, it's best not to be the sole owner. Include one or more other Members, even if they are family members and even if their interests are small.

Provided that a court respects the terms of the operating agreement, the most it is likely to do for the benefit of your creditor is to issue a "charging order." The charging order tells the LLC that if and when it makes a distribution that otherwise would be payable to you, it must make the payment to your creditor. This would temporarily block you from benefiting directly from the LLC; on the other hand, it wouldn't put a dime into the creditor's pocket, since you as Manager would simply refrain from making distributions to the Members.

The result would be a waiting game between you and the creditor. You wouldn't like being forced to play the game, but you would find it far preferable to simply having your assets swept away. And it would position you to negotiate a favorable settlement with the creditor, who is likely to be far less patient than you.

## Good Practice

There are two other steps that will encourage any court to respect your LLC as an entity that is separate and distinct from you. They are especially important if you are the only Member.

- Manage the LLC as though it were owned by someone else — someone to whom you were responsible. Always follow the Operating Agreement. Never pay your personal bills out of the LLC's checking account. If the company reimburses you for expenses you actually and reasonably incurred on the company's behalf, provide the company with receipts for those expenses.

- Use the LLC for purposes other than asset protection, such as international investing.

## U.S. Income Tax Treatment of Foreign LLCs

(If you're not a U.S. taxpayer, you may want to skip this section and jump to "Non-U.S. Tax Treatment of Foreign LLCs.")

U.S. income tax rules are remarkably accommodating for LLCs. An LLC is given leeway in choosing how it will be treated.

**No affirmative election.** Regardless of how many Members it has, a foreign LLC is classified as a foreign corporation for all U.S. income tax purposes — unless it files Form 8832 with the IRS to make an affirmative election to be classified otherwise. Assuming that you intend to use your foreign LLC to hold investments (and not to run a business), you almost certainly should file an election to have the LLC treated either as a partnership or as a disregarded entity (i.e., a sole proprietorship).

**Partnership treatment.** If there is more than one distinct Member (such as an LLC owned partly by you and partly by one of your children), the company can elect to be treated as a partnership. As such, the company would file a partnership tax return each year. Then you as a Member would include your share of the company's income, gains, deductions, and credits on your personal tax return, and each of the other Members would include his share of those items on his own personal return.

There generally is no income tax on transferring assets to an LLC that has elected partnership treatment. However, if you transfer stocks, bonds, or other securities that are worth more than you paid for them, and if more than 80% of the company's assets consist of cash and securities, and if the result is that you diversify your holdings to even a modest degree (because another Member contributed something different), you will recognize any built-in gain on the transfer, just as though you had sold the securities.

There generally is no income tax on distributions from an LLC that has elected partnership treatment. However, if the total distributions you receive ever exceeds the total of: (1) the cash you transferred to the LLC, plus (2) the cost of the investments you transferred to the LLC, plus (3) your cumulative share of the LLC's net income, any excess will be a capital gain.

**Disregarded entity.** If the LLC is owned by just one distinct Member, such as you as an individual, it can elect to be a "disregarded entity." In that case, the LLC doesn't file an income tax return; instead, you would include all of the company's income, deductions, and credits on your own tax return. It's as though the company is simply a financial account that you own.

Even if an LLC has more than one Member, if all the Members are indistinct from one another for income tax purposes, the LLC nonetheless can elect to be a disregarded entity (and may not be eligible to be treated as a partnership). For example...

If the LLC is partly owned by you and partly owned by your revocable living trust (which, for income tax purposes, would be a "grantor trust" that is indistinct from you), and if there are no other owners, the LLC is eligible to be a disregarded entity. Or if the LLC is owned partly by you personally and partly by a trust for your children that includes provisions that make it your grantor trust, the LLC is eligible to be a disregarded entity.

You can transfer assets of any kind to a foreign LLC that is your own disregarded entity without triggering any income tax consequences — even if the assets are highly appreciated. For income tax purposes, you are transferring the property to yourself. Distributions work the same way; a distribution by the LLC to you has no income tax consequences because (for income tax purposes) you are transferring property to yourself.

**Funding by you and your spouse.** An LLC that is owned entirely by husband and wife as community property can elect either to be treated as a partnership or, if husband and wife file a joint income tax return, as a disregarded entity. So if an LLC is funded solely by community property (contributed by you and your spouse), it can elect either to be disregarded or to be a partnership. However, if any interest in the LLC derives from separate property, the LLC may not be eligible to be a disregarded entity and except in unusual cases should elect to be a partnership.

If you live in a community property state and either you or your spouse wants to transfer what is now separate property to the LLC, consider first entering into a "transmutation agreement." A transmutation agreement is a simple legal instrument (sometimes just one page) by which husband and wife agree that specified items of separate property shall be transmuted into community property. This would allow you to fund the LLC solely with community property and thereby allow the LLC to be a disregarded entity.

If you do not live in a community property state and both you and your spouse want to transfer what is now separate property to the LLC, the LLC can elect to be treated as a partnership. Assuming that most of the LLC's assets will consist of cash and securities, contributions by you and your spouse of nonmatching sets of appreciated property could trigger capital gains tax. However, you can avoid the potential for tax if before making the contribution, each of you makes a gift of a 50% interest in the separate property to the other spouse. Doing so would eliminate the potential for tax by preventing the transfers to the LLC from effecting a diversification of assets for either of you.

If you aren't certain whether an LLC funded by both you and your spouse is eligible to elect to be a disregarded entity, you should consult with a tax attorney or accountant. If you cannot arrive at a clear answer to the question, to avoid uncertainty and to eliminate the risk that the LLC might fall into the default classification of corporation, the LLC should elect to be a partnership.

See Chapter 12 for important information on the IRS reporting requirements that come with a foreign LLC.

# U.S. Estate Planning with a Foreign LLC

A now-standard device for reducing gift and estate tax is to repackage assets in ways that reduce their "fair market value." Since gift and estate taxes are levied on fair market value, the repackaging can achieve a reduction in tax. More complex strategies can build on such "valuation discounts" to completely protect even a very large estate from the tax collector.

In applying the repackaging device to an LLC, assets are transferred to the LLC in exchange for a membership interest. After the LLC has been funded, its Operating Agreement is amended to include provisions — such as non-transferability — that make a non-controlling membership interest economically unattractive to any third party, i.e., the provisions reduce the fair market value of a non-controlling interest. Non-controlling interests are then given or sold at discounted prices to family members or placed in trust for them.

A foreign LLC can be used in this way and may allow more flexibility than a domestic LLC, since certain jurisdictions (as explained below) allow even a 99% membership interest to be non-controlling.

# Non-U.S. Tax Treatment of Foreign LLCs

Tax rules in most countries, including Canada, treat a foreign limited liability company as though it were a foreign corporation. So a threshold question for a non-U.S. investor considering the use of a foreign LLC is, "Would there be any serious tax disadvantage to investing through a foreign corporation?" If the answer is in the affirmative, you can strike foreign LLCs from your list of possibilities. But if there would be no tax disadvantages to using a foreign corporation, you may want to use an LLC instead, for lower cost and more convenient operation.

# Opening Accounts

Opening bank and brokerage accounts for your LLC will be part of your job as Manager. To make the job easier, the LLC's operating agreement should explicitly authorize the Manager to open and operate such accounts.

Each institution that you approach to establish an account will ask for the same information and documentation about you as Manager that would be required for a personal account — including a notarized copy of your passport and a utility bill or other evidence linking you to a residential address. In addition, for the LLC itself, the institution will want a certified copy of the LLC's articles of formation, a certified copy of the operating agreement, and a certificate of incumbency representing that you are in fact the LLC's Manager. Expect variation from institution to institution in the names given to the required documents, and expect variation as to what "certified" means.

Also be prepared for some confusion. The personnel in many institutions outside the U.S. are hazy on the LLC concept. When it does come into focus for them, they're likely to see it as a variant form of corporation. Don't waste any effort trying to explain that it isn't.

## Choice of Jurisdiction

Limited liability companies are authorized by the laws of Cook Islands, Nevis, Anguilla, and Belize.

Of the four jurisdictions, Cook Islands is the most notable in that its Limited Liability Companies Act is largely a reproduction of the Delaware law authorizing limited liability companies. The Cook Islands law has two important features. First, a charging order is the only remedy available to a creditor of a Member. Thus, the Cook Islands courts will not force an LLC to accept a Member's creditor as a substitute owner of a membership interest. Second, an Operating Agreement may require a supermajority or even unanimity for key actions, such as liquidating the company, replacing the Manager, or amending the Operating Agreement.

No jurisdiction has an LLC law that is more helpful than what the Cook Islands parliament has enacted. And the Cook Islands is a socially healthier place than the three other jurisdictions.

If you're located on the Atlantic Seaboard and want a jurisdiction that is closer to home, consider Nevis. Its LLC law is virtually identical to that of the Cook Islands.

# — 9 —

# INTERNATIONAL TRUSTS

You can go a long way toward safety just by using the relatively simple measures discussed so far.

- A foreign bank account for protection from a paralyzing, lightning seizure of your financial assets in the U.S. and for independence from the U.S. dollar.

- Gold safely stored in multiple locations to protect against a disruptive breakdown of the world's fiat money system.

- Stocks in companies based outside the US, so that you're less dependent on the health of the U.S. economy.

- A foreign LLC to give you greater access to international markets and to serve as a stronger barrier to lawsuit predators.

Put those devices to work and you will be in much better shape — far more secure — than most of the people you know. But you may want to go a step further, to eliminate your remaining vulnerability.

There's a limitation inherent in all the methods and strategies for improving your financial safety that have been discussed so far: you. You own the bank account and the gold and the foreign stocks. And you own and manage the foreign LLC. Thus any government agency that can get to you can get to the wealth you're trying to protect.

What happens when the Patriotic Gold Act of 2016 or the Currency Stabilization Act of 2017 requires you to sell your foreign assets to the government at prices the government sets? What happens when a judge tells you exactly how you are going to manage your foreign LLC?

Almost any other asset you own, no matter what its character or location, shares the same vulnerability. You own it, so even if it affords you a valuable opportunity for foot-dragging or strengthens your bargaining position with a lawsuit assailant, or even if the next wonderful idea out of Washington overlooks it, you can be compelled eventually to hand it over.

## Ownership for Others

There's a startling corollary to this. The only way to achieve complete protection for your wealth is to let someone else own it for you! Nothing I might say on the topic could provoke more psychological resistance than that short message. But if you're going to gain all the asset protection you want, it's a message you need to hear. The only way to complete the circle of safety for your wealth is to let someone own it for you.

If giving up direct personal ownership seems like an unacceptably drastic step, consider what outright ownership has come to mean for an American in the 21st century.

Ownership means keeping assets available for anyone who wins a lawsuit against you.

Ownership means that when a government agency imposes a penalty on you or merely enrolls you in a category of designated bad people, there is something for it to take.

Ownership means that if a government agency wants the particular thing you own — such as gold or silver — it knows the name and address of the person to squeeze.

Ownership means that when the government imposes controls on where or how capital can be invested, your wealth is part of the program.

Ownership means that you're liable for tax on the income from the property.

Ownership means that the government may eventually take more of your wealth than it leaves behind for your heirs.

Direct personal ownership just isn't what it used to be. In today's environment, the closest you can get to the benefits of real ownership is to let someone else do the owning for you.

Of course, to even consider letting someone else take on the role of owner, you first would have to see that the arrangement is just right. Precisely and unmistakably right. Precisely and unmistakably reliable. In particular, you would need to be absolutely confident that the new owner would always use the assets for your benefit and for the benefit of the other people you want to provide for.

You would be asking the new owner to take on the job of owner-for-others. And you would be counting on the new owner to perform its job efficiently and faithfully.

It's a tall order, but at the risk of repetition, such an arrangement is the only way to approach absolute protection for your wealth. So let's figure out how to make it work.

## Irrevocable and Discretionary

Two features are essential if the arrangement between you and the new owner (the owner-for-others) is going to truly safeguard your wealth.

To shut out all possible attackers, the arrangement must be irrevocable. Suppose that you retained the right simply to tell the owner-for-others to return everything to you. In that case, any court or other government agency could compel you to exercise that right. Then you'd have no choice but to give up the assets on the government's terms. So it's a right you mustn't have.

And the arrangement must give the owner-for-others an element of discretion. Neither you nor anyone else you've provided for in the arrangement should have a fixed, individual claim on the assets you've handed over to the owner-for-others. While the owner-for-others would be obligated to use the assets only for you or for other persons you've included, none of you should have a right to demand, say, half the capital or a quarter of the income. If you had such a right, a court could order you to assign that right to the winner of a lawsuit or to a government agency collecting a tax, enforcing a penalty or scooping foreign currencies or other assets held outside the US.

Instead of fixed rights, you and the other persons you've included should merely be eligible to receive benefits. Notice the implication: the owner-for-others would be taking on the responsibility to judge which of the people you've included gets what, when he gets it, and how he gets it.

Irrevocable and discretionary. The combination is extremely powerful. It erects a stone wall, since no arm of government and no private party can take from you what you neither own nor can demand to receive. And in the long run, it presents an unsolvable puzzle for tax collectors. The tax collector may tax you personally on the income from the transferred property, and it may include the property in your taxable estate, but after your lifetime, there is no way to attribute any further income to any of your heirs or to treat the property as part of any other person's taxable estate.

Irrevocable and discretionary. The combination isn't just one of many possible formulas to choose from. The combination is a necessity, an essential, an absolute prerequisite for achieving the highest level of robust asset protection. There is no other way to get there.

Irrevocable and discretionary...so powerful, yet so hard to accept. Even if I've succeeded in showing why those two features are both powerful and necessary for someone looking to protect his wealth, almost no one would hand his assets over to an owner-for-others if there weren't more to the story. How can you be sure the owner-for-others will pay attention to your needs and wants and will respond intelligently to the changing circumstances of the other persons you've included? Maybe the owner-for-others will go to sleep...or forget your name...or walk away with your money.

Troubling questions indeed. But the combination of irrevocable and discretionary is the only way to get your wealth completely out of the system that threatens to take it. So we need to find a way to make that combination acceptable and worry-free. You'll be happy to know there is, indeed, such a way. And it has been used successfully for generations by many of the world's wealthiest families.

## The Basis for Confidence

Here are the preliminary ingredients for confidence:

> **Location.** The laws where the new owner is located should respect and enforce the concept of ownership-for-others and should encourage its use.
>
> **Respect** for the concept means that under local law, the assets would not be available either to your creditors or to the new owner's creditors.
>
> **Enforcement** means that the owner-for-others takes on a legal duty to use the assets to carry out your purposes and intentions, so that you or any other person you've included would have standing to sue the owner-for-others for failing to live up to its duty.
>
> **Encouragement** means that the income from the property you transfer won't be taxed in the country where the owner-for-others is located, nor will the property ever be subject to gift or estate tax in that country.
>
> **Documentation.** The arrangement should be spelled out in a legally binding document. Who is included in the "others" the new owner is promising to look out for? How do investment decisions get made? Is there someone who monitors the performance of the owner-for-others? Can you replace the owner-for-others if its performance is unsatisfactory? Can you move the arrangement to a different country if conditions change?
>
> **Continuity.** The owner-for-others should be an institution, not an individual. Individuals get sick. They die, sometimes unexpectedly. You know how individuals in general tend to behave, but you never know how any particular individual might

behave. People are too complicated, with too many motives. You need an institution. And it should be an institution that's in the business of being an owner-for-others.

**Stake.** The institution that takes on the job of owner-for-others should have something serious at stake, something that it would put at risk by not living up to its responsibilities. It should have a valuable reputation that it wants to protect. It should have financial capital that it could lose if it failed to keep its promises. It should be earning a fee for serving as owner-for-others, an income source it wouldn't want to lose.

# A Hammer in Your Hand

Those factors are a good start, but the real hammer ensuring good performance by the owner-for-others is the monitor. Someone, probably you, should have a right to monitor every aspect of the arrangement and to give advice that the owner-for-others would be obligated to listen to and consider.

**Reliance.** The owner-for-others should be permitted to rely on the advice it receives from the monitor except when it would be clearly unreasonable to do so, including advice on investment decisions and on sending money to you or any of the other persons you've included.

**Right to replace.** The monitor should have a power to fire the owner-for-others and replace it with a different institution.

**Path of succession.** The monitor should have a power to appoint his own successor, so that there always will be a monitor.

To see how the monitor's powers (powers you probably will want to hold personally) ensure good performance by the owner-for-others, consider things from the point of view of the institution you've selected for the job. What does the institution want?

1.  The institution serving as owner-for-others wants to collect its fee every year. It knows that won't happen for long if you as

monitor become dissatisfied and switch to a different institution.

2.   It wants to avoid getting sued by you or any of the other people you've included. An easy way to do that is to rely on the advice it gets from you as monitor. The owner-for-others knows that it's protected when it follows the monitor's advice.

3.   It wants peace and quiet, and it wants to protect its reputation. Two more reasons for the owner-for-others to pay attention to the monitor.

Add it all up. The monitor has no power to order the owner-for-others to hand money or other assets over to anyone, so the money is safe — no one can force you as monitor to access the assets the owner-for-others is holding. Yet as monitor you have profound influence over the owner-for-others and how it uses the assets for you and the other persons you've included.

There's one more element of confidence to consider. How can you be sure the owner-for-others won't steal? Of course, you would choose an institution to be your owner-for-others only after carefully considering its qualifications and reputation. But you don't need to rely solely on your due-diligence investigation.

In addition, you can insert an impenetrable layer of financial control by using a limited liability company. The only thing the owner-for-others would own is the interest in the LLC. The LLC — not the owner-for-others — would own the assets you want to protect. And you (or someone else you recommend) would be the LLC's Manager.

As Manager, you would have financial and investment control over all the assets. It would be impossible for an unethical owner-for-others to steal anything. In addition, to allow for the possibility that a court or other government agency someday might want to compel you to use your management powers against your wishes, the LLC structure could include a Standby Manager of your choosing. The Standby Manager would step in automatically if you ever decide that you no longer want to be the Manager.

## Something More Familiar

By now you've probably noticed that the terms I've been using are descriptive but roundabout phrases for more customary language. The thousand-year-old term for "ownership for others" is "trust." The rest of the expressions line up as follows:

Owner-for-others = Trustee

Legally binding document = trust instrument (or trust deed)

You transferring assets = You as Grantor of the trust

You and other included persons = Beneficiaries of the trust

You as monitor = You as Trust Protector (or simply Protector)

Assets you transfer = trust fund

The type of trust I've been describing is usually called an international asset protection trust or simply an international trust. For the reasons I've explained, it is the only arrangement that can achieve truly robust protection for family wealth, because it puts just enough legal distance between you and the assets you want to protect. The advantages you achieve with an international trust are:

**Brick wall against lawsuits.** Provided that you're solvent when you transfer assets to the Trustee, you can make it impossible for any lawsuit predator ever to reach them.

**Shut out any sudden asset seizures.** Because the assets are held by a non-US trust company, they can't be seized by any U.S. government agency.

**Avoid U.S. investment controls or gold confiscation.** Your trust will be outside the range of any investment restriction, capital controls, or program of gold confiscation the U.S. government might undertake.

**Investment freedom.** Neither your trust nor the LLC it owns is a U.S. person, so they're both welcome as customers at many institutions that turn away individual Americans.

**Income tax advantages.** An international trust may give you access to income tax planning opportunities that aren't available to most investors in the US. And after your lifetime, the trust completely disconnects from the U.S. income tax system. Then no one in the U.S. will be subject to tax on the trust's income.

**Estate-planning advantages.** Everything you might do at home to reduce or eliminate estate tax can also be done with an international trust — and more. With an international trust, it is possible to get wealth out of your taxable estate and still keep it available for your support, which makes the trust the ideal environment for estate planning and whittling your family's exposure to estate tax down to zero. An even greater advantage in the long run is that after your personal estate is settled, the trust disconnects from the U.S. estate tax system. It needn't be in the taxable estate of any of your heirs.

**Privacy.** You personally will be required to report the trust (so make sure your tax accountant knows what you're doing). But after your lifetime, the trust can be lawfully silent and lawfully invisible.

## Why Not

The advantages of an international trust are so enormous that you might wonder why so few people have one. After three decades of experience in financial planning, I believe I know the answer.

Yes, there is widespread desire for the safety and tax-planning advantages of an international trust — but until you've done your homework, the idea of establishing one can seem dauntingly exotic and adventuresome. And there are a series of worries — How can I trust the trustee? Will I be painting a target on my back for the IRS? Won't it be terribly complex and expensive? — that get in the way. None of these concerns have a firm basis in fact, but any of them might hold you back.

# 10

# A BRIDGE FAR ENOUGH

A second passport protects you from being locked in. Without it, your government can effectively place you under house arrest by taking back the passport it gave you. To obtain a second passport, you first must obtain a second citizenship.

Among other things, having a second passport allows you to invest, bank, travel, reside, and do business in places that you couldn't before.

More options means more freedom and opportunity.

Obtaining a second citizenship and passport is a prudent goal for anyone, from a Westerner seeking to insulate himself from the increasingly desperate measures of bankrupt governments to a Middle Easterner looking to escape a conflict zone without having to live like a refugee.

The benefits of a second passport include:

**"Bolt-hole" access.** A second passport is a mobility insurance policy for you and your family. Regardless of how bad the situation may get in your native country, with a second passport you'll always have the right to live elsewhere and perhaps in several other countries (an EU passport gives you 28 countries from which to choose).

**Disassociation with your native country.** Certain passports may attract negative attention in some parts of the world, notably passports from the US, Britain, France, and Israel.

If your home government has developed a bad habit of sticking its nose in the affairs of other nations, you could be a target should you happen to be in the wrong place at the wrong time.

There are, of course, passports that carry minimal foreign policy blowback risk. For example, when was the last time you saw Swiss passport holders targeted?

**Wider visa-free travel.** A passport is as good as the level of visa-free travel it affords — the ability to go where you choose without applying in advance for a visa. Also, a second passport may help you avoid entry fees and other travel restrictions. For example, Brazil, Chile, and Argentina all collect a visa fee (of about US$160) from travelers who present a U.S. passport. U.S. passport holders are singled out for the fee because the American government imposes a similar charge on citizens from the annoyed countries when they enter the US.

Finnish and Swedish passports offer visa-free travel to the greatest number of countries. Afghanistan, not surprisingly, issues one of the least useful passports.

> **Do Passport Holders from Country X Need a Visa to Enter Country Y?** VisaHQ (https://www.visahq.com/citizens/) shows the travel restrictions and visa requirements for various combinations of passports and destinations.

**More Financial Options.** A second passport unlocks the door to international financial services. This is especially true for Americans. Due to the long reach of U.S. regulators, most (but not yet all) foreign financial institutions now turn away anyone who presents a U.S. passport. To be a welcome customer, you need to present a passport from a different country.

**Expatriation.** You cannot effectively renounce your U.S. citizenship unless you hold citizenship in another country.

## Permissibility

U.S. law allows dual citizenship, but not all countries do the same. Some countries discourage it, some rigorously ban it, and still others have banning laws they do little to enforce.

Laws in the following countries prohibit or severely restrict dual citizenship:

| | | |
|---|---|---|
| Algeria | Iraq | Palau |
| Andorra | Japan | Papua |
| Azerbaijan | Kazakhstan | Príncipe Island |
| Bahrain | Kuwait | Qatar |
| Belarus | Kyrgyzstan | Rwanda |
| Bhutan | Laos | Saudi Arabia |
| Bolivia | Libya | Sierra Leone |
| Botswana | Malawi | Singapore |
| Brunei | Malaysia | South Korea |
| Burundi | Mali | Sudan |
| Cameroon | Monaco | Swaziland |
| China | Mongolia | Sweden |
| Congo | Myanmar | Tonga |
| Cuba | Nepal | Uganda |
| Djibouti | New Guinea | Ukraine |
| Equatorial Guinea | Nicaragua | United Arab Emirates |
| Gabon | Niger | Uzbekistan |
| Guinea | North Korea | Venezuela |
| Honduras | Norway | Vietnam |
| India | Paraguay | Yemen |
| Indonesia | Pakistan | Zimbabwe |

Under Title 8 of the U.S. Code, a U.S. citizen who takes a second citizenship won't lose his U.S. citizenship. Two Supreme Court decisions (*Afroyim vs. Rusk*, 1967 and *Vance vs. Terrazas*, 1980) have upheld the permissibility of dual citizenship. A second citizenship wouldn't compromise your status as a U.S. citizen, nor would it alter your U.S. obligations in any way.

## Routes to a Second Passport

There are exactly three legitimate routes to obtaining a second citizenship and passport. If you hear about a fourth route, assume that you're hearing about a scam. Black- and gray-market passports (most commonly from Bulgaria, Mexico, Paraguay, and Cambodia) are much more trouble than they're worth and should be avoided.

Some passport scams, such as the selling of alleged "diplomatic passports," are obvious. Others that involve gray-market passports are less obvious but equally dangerous.

Black-market passports — stolen, cloned, or counterfeit documents — are completely illegitimate and are the stuff of organized crime and spy agencies. While it's not impossible that you will run across black-market passports in your search for a legit second passport, it also is not very likely.

Gray-market passports, on the other hand, are far more common and can appear legitimate, which makes it even more important for you to be able to identify them.

A gray-market passport is an officially issued document that was obtained (usually with the help of a bribed local official) by skirting the legal requirements for naturalization. If a service provider talks about a "special friend" in a foreign government who can help you get a passport faster and easier than by following the rules, things are looking gray.

No matter the country, you should be able to point to *specific* naturalization laws with *explicitly defined* requirements that clearly spell out everything. This information is usually located on the government's website or the website of a consulate or embassy.

If you cannot independently verify the information someone gives you with the government in question, or if what you're being told doesn't match what you know about the legal requirements, consider the discrepancy a **major red flag**. In all likelihood, someone is attempting to sell you a bogus passport — one that is expensive but dangerous and perhaps worthless.

This is especially true of providers that hype little-known economic citizenship programs. There are exactly two untroubled economic citizenship programs that have stood the test of time (see below), and they're governed by laws that are public knowledge. It's the ones that don't come with clear laws outlining the program and its costs that you have to watch out for.

Unfortunately, there is no route to obtaining a genuine second passport that is fast, easy, and cheap.

Unless you have sufficient money for an economic citizenship program, have ancestry in certain countries, or are willing to make extreme lifestyle decisions (marriage, adoption, military service), expect the process to take at least three to four years. Five years is common. Ten years is not rare. Generally, faster is costlier.

It will help if you view the entire world as your hunting ground. Don't dismiss the idea of becoming a citizen of a small or backward country. Unlike most of the mega-government countries, such places generally lack both the capacity and the desire to monitor their citizens or treat them as though they were the government's property.

> Treat with skepticism anyone who claims to have a "special friend" in a foreign government who can provide a shortcut to a second passport.

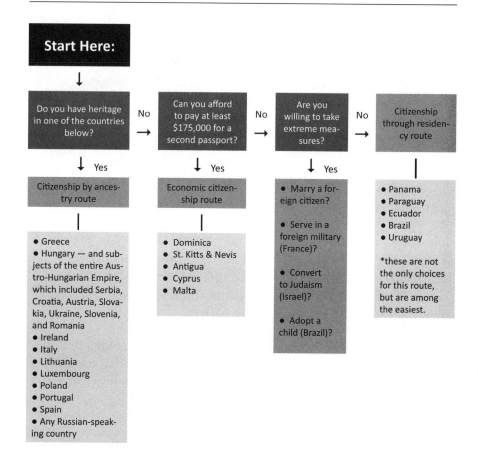

## 1. Citizenship by Ancestry

If you qualify, the fastest and least costly method for obtaining a second passport is through a citizenship-by-ancestry program.

Within the European Union, some of the countries that offer citizenship to descendants of natives are:

- Italy

- Ireland

- Poland

- Greece

- Lithuania

- Luxembourg

- Portugal

- Spain

- Hungary (which opens the door to descendants of subjects of the entire Austro-Hungarian Empire, which included Serbia, Croatia, Austria, Slovakia, Ukraine, Slovenia, and Romania).

Russia has relaxed its requirements for obtaining citizenship for those who are fluent in Russian and live or have lived in the Soviet Union or the former Russian Empire or have parents or grandparents who lived in those areas. Get in touch with the nearest Russian embassy or consulate for details.

Each country has its own eligibility requirements and procedures. If you have an ancestor who hailed from one of those countries (usually not more remote than a great-grandparent), you should find citizenship information on the country's website, or you can visit a consulate.

If you determine that you're eligible, you will then need to give the consulate official legal and translated documents (birth certificates, marriage certificates, death certificates, naturalization records, etc.) proving lineage to the relevant ancestor.

After you've submitted the complete application for citizenship, it generally will take three to six months for the consulate and government to process and approve the application. When you've become a citizen, you will then be eligible to apply for a passport.

## 2. Economic Citizenship Programs

Economic citizenship is the most expensive but also the quickest route to a second passport. You make a substantial payment or investment, and in return the government grants you full and permanent citizenship. It all can be done in a matter of weeks, and there is no need ever to reside in the country.

Currently, the governments of Dominica and St. Kitts & Nevis (two English-speaking countries in the Caribbean) offer the only established and reliable economic citizenship programs available today. A passport from either government enables visa-free entry to most of Latin America, the Caribbean, and Europe.

The payments required under each program are detailed below. You should expect to incur additional costs, such as due diligence, background checks, processing, and other fees that all in all may exceed US$10,000 per person.

Other countries also offer economic citizenship programs. These programs, however, have not been around nearly as long as the ones from Dominica and St. Kitts.

The lack of a reliable and stable history is an important distinction to consider between programs. Ultimately, any government has the authority to revoke the passport and/or citizenship of any of its citizens at any time for any reason, real or concocted. A shift in the political winds could mean that an economic citizenship program that was in favor today may be out of favor tomorrow...with negative consequences for those who participated in the program.

An economic citizenship program must have an established record of credibility, and that comes in part from a history of domestic political acceptance. Only the St. Kitts and Dominica programs have stood the test of time (decades) and been successfully used by thousands of people.

**Dominica**

The economic citizenship program of Dominica (not to be confused with the Dominican Republic) entails a nonrefundable donation to the government.

Dominica imposes an income tax on its citizens, but only if they reside in the country. Nonresident citizens are not subject to income tax.

The donation schedule is:

- US$175,000 for an individual

- US$225,000 for a married couple

- US$225,000 for a couple with two children under the age of 18, plus US$50,000 for each additional child.

Dominica also offers an option to invest in approved real estate projects as an additional path to citizenship (in addition to the donation option).

For more information, consult with the nearest consulate or embassy of Dominica.

## St. Kitts & Nevis

The St. Kitts & Nevis program involves either making a donation to the government or purchasing a villa or condo from an approved developer.

If you choose the donation option, the schedule is:

- US$250,000 for a single applicant

- US$300,000 for an applicant, spouse, and up to two children under age 18

- US$350,000 for an applicant, spouse, and up to four children under age 18

If you chose the real estate option, the amount you invest in approved real estate must be at least:

- US$400,000 for the applicant

- US$25,000 for the applicant's spouse and for each dependent under the age of 18

- US$50,000 for each dependent over the age of 18

For dependents over 18 years, an additional fee of $50,000 is payable to the government. In addition, the government requires a fee of 4-5% of the real estate purchase price.

You must hold the property for at least five years. If you sell before that, you can lose your citizenship (and passport). Selling after five years would not compromise your status.

The real estate option entails a higher out-of-pocket cost than simply making a donation to the government. On the other hand, you would be buying something of real value (a condo on the Caribbean, for example).

St. Kitts & Nevis imposes no income tax on its citizens, i.e., there would be no tax consequences to taking up residency in the country.

## Cyprus

The Cyprus economic citizenship program also gets you an EU passport, but it's a much more expensive option at a minimum of €2.5 million.

The previous minimum investment amount for obtaining Cypriot citizenship was €10 million, but following the crisis, the government cut the price and added several options. To qualify, you must have a clean criminal record and own a private residence in Cyprus worth at least €500,000.

The four paths to citizenship by investment in Cyprus are:

1. Make an investment and a donation consisting of:

    a. €2 million investment into eligible companies; and

    b. €500,000 donation to a government fund.

2. Invest €5 million in eligible companies or real estate.

3. Make a €5 million fixed-term deposit in a Cypriot bank (minimum of three years).

4.  Be a person who lost €3 million from the bail-in.

# 3. Other Paths to Naturalization: Qualifying Circumstances

Another path to naturalization is to obtain and then maintain permanent resident status for an extended period (with or without actual presence in the jurisdiction). The required term may be as brief as three years (Paraguay) or as long as 20 years (Andorra). Most countries will grant citizenship after five years or so of permanent residency.

Qualifying circumstances include marriage, which in most cases requires you to be married for at least two years. France grants citizenship upon completion of military service. A Jew is eligible for Israeli citizenship, though in most cases military service will be required of any applicant over the age of 18.

The requirements for obtaining citizenship through residency vary from country to country. Some factors you should weigh in considering a country's program:

- Required length of residency

- Minimum time required in-country during residency period

- Costs and/or mandatory investments

- Requirement to demonstrate language proficiency

- Permissibility of dual citizenship.

Below are details on some of the more appealing countries to consider for resident status and eventual citizenship. As a resident of a foreign country, you will likely be inducted into its tax system. Though the list is not comprehensive and the requirements are constantly changing, the material should give you a good idea of what to expect.

# Countries to Consider for Naturalization by Residency

For specific professional contacts to assist with residency, citizenship, and naturalization, please see Chapter 13.

## *Argentina*

The Argentine constitution says that after only two years of uninterrupted permanent residency, you can become an Argentine national.

The process to apply for residency involves showing that you have enough resources to maintain yourself, or that you have been offered a job in Argentina. There are other ways as well. It can take up to two years to get permanent residency status, and then two years after that you can be eligible for Argentine citizenship.

## *Ecuador*

Ecuador offers one of the shortest routes to naturalization. After just three years of resident status, you're eligible to be naturalized.

In total, it will take around four years when you consider the time to process the residency and naturalization requests.

You must apply for resident status while in the country and remain there for four to six weeks while your request is processed.

The easiest way to obtain resident status is to purchase a US$25,000 CD from a local bank or make a minimum US$25,000 investment in real estate. Both options require that you maintain your investment in order to keep your residency status.

During the first year of residency, you cannot be out of the country for more than 90 days. After completing the first-year residency requirement, you cannot be out of the country for more than 18 months in years two and three. After completing the three years of residency and approximately another year of processing, you become eligible for an Ecuadorian passport. With passport in hand, you can liquidate the original US$25,000 investment and leave the country as you please.

Ecuador generally recognizes dual citizenship; you shouldn't need to give up your native passport.

## *Brazil*

The first step toward Brazilian citizenship is to obtain resident status.

Perhaps the easiest way to obtain resident status is through the economic residency program that requires a minimum investment of 150,000 Brazilian reals in a business.

Once permanent resident status is established, the time to citizenship is four years, or less if one of the special factors below applies. Full-time residence in the country during the four years is not required. Entering the country at least once every two years generally is sufficient to maintain resident status and stay on the path to citizenship. Naturalization requires demonstrating proficiency in Portuguese.

Factors that can shorten the time to citizenship to as little as one year are:

- Marriage to a Brazilian citizen

- Financial responsibility for a Brazilian child (most likely because you are the parent of a child born in Brazil)

- Citizenship in another country where Portuguese is an official language.

Brazil allows dual citizenship, so there is no need to give up your native passport.

A Brazilian passport gives visa-free travel to many countries, which soon will include the US. The Brazilian government will not extradite a citizen to a foreign country for any reason.

## Panama

A relatively new law (Executive Decree 343) makes obtaining permanent residency in Panama relatively easy for citizens of 47 specific countries which "maintain friendly, professional, economic, and investment relationships with the Republic of Panama." This program is often referred to as the "Specific Countries" or "Friendly Countries" program.

It requires one simple application and a deposit of at least $5,000 in a local bank account, plus an additional sum of $2,000 for each dependent. Applicants will also have to show proof of some meaningful economic activity in Panama, such as ownership of Panamanian real estate or corporation, or an employment contract from a business in Panama.

Once you've obtained permanent residence, you become eligible to eventually obtain full citizenship after five years.

Eligible countries include: Andorra, Argentina, Australia, Austria, Belgium, Brazil, Canada, Chile, Croatia, Cyprus, Czech Republic, Denmark, Estonia, Finland, France, Germany, Greece, Hong Kong, Hungary, Ireland, Israel, Japan, Latvia, Liechtenstein, Lithuania, Luxembourg, Malta, Monaco, Marino, Montenegro, Netherlands, New Zealand, Norway, Poland, Portugal, Serbia, Singapore, Slovakia, Spain, South Africa, South Korea, Sweden, Switzerland, Taiwan, USA, Uruguay, and the UK.

Although Panama does not officially recognize dual citizenship, you don't have to give up your previous passport/citizenship when you become naturalized.

## Paraguay

Paraguay offers one of the easiest and cheapest ways to obtain permanent resident status and a relatively short path to naturalization.

The process for obtaining residence includes presenting a birth certificate, police record, and other documents translated into Spanish and certified to a Paraguayan consulate or embassy. After submitting the documents, the application for residency must be submitted in person in Paraguay. The applicant must also open a local bank account with at least US$5,500.

Once resident status is granted — it can take up to six months — you must be in the country to pick up your national ID card (*cédula*). The issuance of a *cédula* can take an additional 2 to 3 months.

You can apply for citizenship three years after the *cédula* has been granted. Although there's no strict requirement to live in Paraguay, it's advisable to spend some time there to demonstrate a tie to the country.

Though Paraguay prohibits dual citizenship for naturalized persons, enforcement is not consistent.

### *Uruguay*

Obtaining resident status takes longer in Uruguay than in other Latin American countries, typically 10-12 months, and you must apply from within the country.

Presence in the country while you wait for your resident status is not required, but spending at least six months within the country is recommended.

Once you receive resident status, you can apply for naturalization after three years if you're married or five years if single. You must spend at least half of each of those years in Uruguay.

Uruguay permits dual citizenship.

## Economic Residency Programs

There are economic residency programs that grant the immediate right to reside in a country, either permanently or for a period of years, in exchange for making a qualifying investment. They are a path — and in some cases a fast track — to eventual citizenship.

Some of the more popular economic or investor residency programs in terms of pursuing a second passport are summarized below.

| | Required Investment | Years to Citizenship | Language Proficiency Required |
|---|---|---|---|
| Cyprus | €300,000 | 5 | No |
| Hungary | €300,000 | 5 | Yes |
| Latvia | €250,000 | 10 | No |
| Portugal | €500,000 | 10 | Yes |
| Brazil | $R150,000 | 4 | Yes |
| Spain | €500,000 | 10 | Yes |
| Colombia | $150,000 | 5 | Yes |
| Malta | €1,150,000 | 1 | No |

# Citizenship for Children

Some countries, including Brazil, Argentina, Canada, Mexico, Chile, and Panama, grant citizenship to a child by virtue of in-country birth. Other countries grant citizenship to children born to foreign parents under certain conditions (i.e., the parents are permanent residents or have lived in the country for a certain amount of time). Australia, New Zealand, the UK, and South Africa are among them.

# Renouncing U.S. Citizenship

The number of Americans renouncing their citizenship is growing and reaching all-time record highs. For many, the benefits of U.S. citizenship no longer outweigh the costs. Whether you're a high-net-worth individual or a young entrepreneur with a lifetime of earnings ahead of you, renouncing your U.S. citizenship is the only way to end your U.S. tax obligations.

Billionaire Eduardo Saverin, cofounder of Facebook, is a noted example. By renouncing his U.S. citizenship, he escaped paying hundreds of millions of dollars in gift and estate tax. He did not, however, escape the so-called Exit Tax (IRS Form 8854 Initial and Annual Expatriation

Statement).

For income tax purposes, you're deemed to have sold everything you own on the day before expatriation at a price equal to its "fair market value." Any appreciation in your investments or home and any deferred income (such as through a traditional IRA or 401(k) plan) becomes taxable.

Intelligent planning can greatly reduce or even eliminate the tax cost of expatriating. Pre-expatriation steps to consider include:

1. Sell your primary residence. Some of the gain on a sale of your primary residence can be tax-free.

2. Transfer your investments to a limited liability company designed to reduce the fair market value of your interest in the LLC. At a minimum, this can eliminate a large portion of the gain that will be subject to the exit tax. It might eliminate all of it.

3. Use the tax-saving strategy explained in Chapter 7 to convert most of your traditional IRA to a Roth IRA.

4. Use an international trust to make "completed gifts" that remove wealth from your taxable estate. Even though the money could be available to you if you need it after you expatriate, any amount that you don't need and that eventually is distributed to U.S. beneficiaries would fall outside the special regime of transfer taxes.

In addition to reducing the exit tax payable by a covered expatriate, steps 2, 3, and 4 may, depending on the numbers, protect you from being classified as a covered expatriate. In that case, expatriation would come without any tax cost.

After you've renounced your U.S. citizenship, you'll be a foreigner when you visit the US. If you have obtained citizenship from one of the 38 visa-waiver program countries listed below, you can enter the U.S. without getting a visa in advance.

The 38 Visa-Waiver Countries

| | | |
|---|---|---|
| Andorra | Hungary | New Zealand |
| Australia | Iceland | Norway |
| Austria | Ireland | Portugal |
| Belgium | Italy | San Marino |
| Brunei | Japan | Singapore |
| Chile | South Korea | Slovakia |
| Czech Republic | Latvia | Slovenia |
| Denmark | Liechtenstein | Spain |
| Estonia | Lithuania | Sweden |
| Finland | Luxembourg | Switzerland |
| France | Malta | Taiwan |
| Germany | Monaco | United Kingdom |
| Greece | Netherlands | |

If you travel with a passport that isn't part of the visa-waiver program, you have to obtain a visa to reenter the US. This usually involves visiting a U.S. consulate or embassy for a personal interview. U.S. tourist visas usually allow a 90-day visit, can be renewed once for an additional 90 days, and are valid for 10 years.

Generally, as a foreigner you can stay in the U.S. for up to 180 days in any year without resuming your career as a U.S. taxpayer.

Renouncing your U.S. citizenship is the only step that will free you from U.S. taxation while you're still breathing. But it's a drastic step that should be taken only after consulting with an attorney.

# 11

# DIVERSIFY YOUR DIGITAL PRESENCE

If you're at all troubled that third parties are accumulating a permanent history of your emails and other electronic communication, then moving your digital presence to a foreign location may provide you some peace of mind while possibly reducing your exposure to the whims of bureaucrats. Doing so is generally the cheapest, easiest, and quickest aspect of internationalization.

Digital internationalization can: hinder the monitoring and tracing of your communications; reduce easy access to your documents that are stored or accessible online; and protect your business or personal websites from being shut down. Internationalization won't make it impossible for snoops to eavesdrop, but it will make life far more difficult for them. You'll no longer be an easy target.

Lessening the visibility of your digital life starts with the most common stores of information on the Web:

- Email

- Online file storage (cloud storage)

- Components of personal/business websites (domain name, server, payment processor)

- IP address (which can point to your physical address).

The overreach of the "War on Terror" lends cover for any U.S. agency to monitor your Internet activity. Draconian copyright laws mean that your personal/business website can be seized at the drop of a hat under the flimsiest of pretexts. Internet service providers and tech companies in the U.S. work hand-in-glove with the U.S. government.

If some part of your digital presence at any time crosses U.S. jurisdiction, you should assume that you have no privacy. That makes this the easiest way to garner some digital protection: just don't conduct any business you wouldn't want a bureaucrat to know about online. Talk about bank accounts, taxes, expatriation, or anything else that you think might be a red flag — take it *offline*. Don't surf websites you don't want others to know about.

In other words, conduct your online life as if it's an open book. Because it is.

It's not a perfect solution, but it certainly is the simplest.

If, however, you want to conduct your online activity a little more freely, you can take steps to keep your trail relatively opaque. With a small amount of setup effort, you can go about your business on the Web as usual, yet know that you're just a little harder to see than most.

### Avoidance = Scrutiny

Note that the very act of taking these steps could raise a red flag against you. If the government is aware which mechanisms avoid most of their surveillance, then they likely scrutinize the people who use those mechanisms. Wouldn't you? That's another argument in favor of simply assuming everything done online is a public record.

## Internationalize/Randomize Your IP Address

Everyone who is connected to the Internet has an IP address which is easily identified and tracked. In most cases, it can literally pinpoint your location.

There are tools available, like virtual private networks (VPNs) and anonymized routing protocols, that enable you to change your IP address and thus mask your actual physical location. Some VPN providers let you select the country in which it will appear you are based. Although most VPNs are fee-based services, free options are available, albeit with limitations.

One of the easiest and cheapest ways (it's free) to browse the Web relatively anonymously is to use Tor, if proper precautions are taken.

It comes as a free combination of tools that includes a customized Firefox browser that will only communicate through the Tor network, so you cannot make any mistakes in accidentally misusing the connection.

Tor is easy to install. It comes as a single download and is as easy to use as any popular Web browser.

There are limitations to using Tor. The connection speed is slow and will significantly limit your ability to download files and watch streaming video.

As an alternative, we suggest you look into Cryptohippie (https://secure. cryptohippie.com/) which masks your IP address and other information that could be used to identify you. Cryptohippie passes all your traffic through its network first, and pledges to keep that network offshore, secure, and free from logging that might come back to haunt you. It's a premium VPN service and very popular among privacy-conscious Internet users.

In addition, if you're in a country that blocks access to certain websites, Cryptohippie or one of its fellow VPN services will get you around this roadblock.

With your searching and general browsing covered, the next thing to consider is the place you keep all your communications.

## Internationalize Your Email

If you want email privacy, it's prudent to internationalize your inbox and use an offshore email account with a provider who has a strong privacy stance and is based in a jurisdiction willing to back it up.

With your mail stored securely offshore, you can take some comfort that the NSA or similar organizations aren't trolling through the storage of your provider to read your messages, looking for activity they might not like.

However, using an email service based in most Western countries provides little, if any, privacy protections. Though there are other jurisdictions that have strong digital privacy laws, Switzerland is a notable standout. The Swiss High Court has ruled that a user's IP address is personal information and protected by the country's strict privacy laws.

Using an offshore email provider in combination with strong, open-source encryption is a significant impediment to anyone who would like to violate your privacy...as long as the person you're emailing with is also using such measures.

An offshore email account isn't always free, though the fees are generally reasonable. Below are some reputable and relatively inexpensive options to consider.

**www.SwissMail.org:** Based in Switzerland.

**www.neomailbox.com:** Also based in Switzerland.

**secure.runbox.com:** Based in Norway, which has strong privacy laws. Runbox is generally considered a cheap and quality option.

**www.e-mail.ph:** Free email provider in the Philippines.

Locating your email offshore is the biggest step you can take to protect it. However, remember that all communications are two-party at the least. No matter how much you do to protect your mail in storage and in transit (all of the above providers ensure your communication with them is secure while you read your mail), all is lost if you communicate with people who don't take the same precautions.

One way to "force" your correspondents into keeping your secrets as secrets is to encrypt the messages you send them. In order for those readers to view the messages, they'll have to decrypt them locally by also installing secure message software on their machines. While it can be a minor inconvenience to get it set up, it works on almost every platform, will keep you more under the radar, and maybe even encourage your contacts to do the same.

With your email now stored safely offshore and your messages transmitted securely even to less-privacy-minded friends and colleagues, the only remaining area of major concern is your documents. Just as with your email, your documents are sitting ducks for online snoops.

## Components for an Online Business

The rise of draconian anti-terrorism laws is widely reported. However, less commonly known is the rise of equally frightening copyright laws. Spurred by media companies with deep pockets and a dreadful fear of technological progress, the most significant risk today lies in the Digital Millennium Copyright Act, which provides rights and obligations to ISPs to take down your website with a mere *unproven* accusation of copyright infringement.

The threat to the host for not complying is significant; thus, action is often taken swiftly and with little or no notice to contest it. There are safe-harbor provisions to protect ISPs. But only those with deep pockets and the courage of their convictions can afford to test them in court.

That's but one of the threats to your operation. Criminal charges, even if unproven, can result in the seizure of websites and their replacement with an FBI or even an Immigration & Customs Enforcement placard. A sure reputation killer, even if you're eventually acquitted.

These may seem like extreme examples, but they're more common than you might think. The government can be judge, jury, and executioner of your business, even if you're just caught up in a simple mistake.

Thankfully, every aspect of your online business can be diversified internationally to lessen the risk of government intrusion or competitors using draconian laws to stifle you under a pile of takedown requests. And you can even extend its reach to new customers around the world.

Here are the three main components of any online business that should be internationalized if you have any concern that such risks might derail your livelihood:

1. **Payment Processors:** With even a whiff of trouble, most merchant account providers and payment processors will quickly shut off service. If the FBI or even the IRS starts asking questions, however innocuously, you might even find yourself shut off and not know why. Your best bet is to have a second (or third) backup operator which you can use to take payments if that happens.

   There are numerous non-U.S. secure-payment processors that will transact payments online. They can process credit card payments in various currencies and transfer the funds to your bank account overseas, or even back in the U.S. in most cases.

   Processor options in Asia include China UnionPay and AliPay; in Europe, there's PayFair. There are many more to be found online with a little searching.

2. **Domain Name:** You might think the global top-level domains (TLDs) like ".com" or ".net" are arbitrated in international courts by the UN or otherwise outside any one country's authority. Unfortunately, it's not the case. The U.S. has jurisdiction over those most common TLDs. This exposes your website to the whims of the U.S. government, which is not shy about seizing domain names. Fortunately, it's easy and cheap to internationalize your domain name.

   Favorable jurisdictions for domain names include the ".co" domain based in Colombia, the ".me" based in Montenegro, or the ".bz" domain run by an entity in Belize.

   While Switzerland is a great place to internationalize some aspects of your digital presence, registering domain names is not one of them. This is because the Swiss ccTLD registrar, Switch, does not allow for domain privacy. If you register a ".ch" domain, your contact information becomes publicly available. Japan's ".jp" TLD has the same issue. However, if you can live with that, they're still great options.

   Marcaria (https://www.marcaria.com/) is a company that offers a convenient way to register multiple global domain names.

3. **Hosting:** When operating an online business, you must also consider where your site will be hosted. Non-U.S. options for website hosting include providers in Switzerland, Panama, Bermuda, Malaysia, and Hong Kong. Providers in these countries will typically not respond to foreign requests regarding a website without a local court order. Combining that with domain internationalization can keep your site online much longer, give you a chance to respond to unfounded accusations, and possibly even let you avoid getting accidentally swept up in some vast dragnet altogether.

   Generally, hosting in a foreign jurisdiction means a slower

website for your customers in the U.S. (and for Google, which accounts for that in search rankings). So if you do go this route, learn about the tricks that allow you to host both in the U.S. and overseas at the same time, so that your site keeps working even if the U.S. portion is knocked out for any reason, from bureaucrat to tornado.

Some offshore webhosts worth checking out:

Orange Website (https://www.orangewebsite.com/) (Iceland)

Icy Evolution (http://www.icyevolution.com/) (Mauritius)

Liberty VPS (https://libertyvps.net/) (Netherlands)

## Keeping Up with the Trend

Internationalization of your digital presence is often overlooked. But just a few simple moves can help mitigate the political risk of subjecting your personal and business life (and possibly your livelihood) to a single, intrusive jurisdiction.

# 12

# FOREIGN ACCOUNT AND ASSET REPORTING

If you're considering internationalizing your financial life, privacy may be one of your goals. Too bad. Because of U.S. reporting rules, you can't have it — at least not to the degree you would like.

The rules are strict, and it would be a mistake to try to operate outside of them. So if you have a general intention to send wealth to another country and hold it there, you should understand the reporting requirements before you formulate a definite plan. And, rather than being a deterrent, understanding the government's reason for the reporting rules should give you a sense of urgency about putting your plan together and then putting it into effect.

Two generations ago, using actual cash (not a check) for large transactions was commonplace. People would buy cars or even houses with hundred-dollar bills. Five-hundred-dollar bills were in general circulation as recently as 1969.

But no longer. Washington wants to know how much money you have and what you're doing with it. The use of cash interferes with that goal. U.S. currency still carries the legend "Legal Tender," but over the last 40 years it has drifted closer and closer toward being illegal tender.

The five-hundred-dollar bill was discontinued at the order of President Nixon, who cited the fight against organized crime as the reason. Since then, other worthy purposes have been recruited as reasons for restricting the use of cash and also for compelling the reporting of financial accounts — the War on Drugs, fighting tax evasion, catching money launderers, and most recently, the War on Terror. Our favorite is the need to protect the public's privacy.

The rules keep changing, almost always in the direction of demanding more information from more people. Here are the reporting rules on cash and international transactions as they stand now.

**Cash transactions.** Within the US, any cash transaction of $10,000 or more must be reported by the financial institution on FinCEN Form 104 (Currency Transaction Report). If you ask to withdraw $10,000 in cash from your bank and the teller calls for his supervisor, Form 104 is the reason.

**Structuring.** The $10,000 rule is supported by a particularly nasty companion, the rule against "structuring." If you make two or more related cash transactions that add up to $10,000 or more, you've structured your affairs to avoid the $10,000 rule — which is a criminal violation. It's analogous to getting pulled over for taking a route that avoids red lights.

**Suspicious transactions.** Your bank is also required to report any "suspicious" transaction, regardless of the amount, on Treasury Department Form 90-22.47 (Suspicious Activity Report).

**Recordkeeping.** Cash purchases of monetary instruments, such as money orders, cashier's checks, and travelers checks totaling from $3,000 to $10,000 must be recorded by the teller in a Monetary Instrument Log. The Log must be kept at the financial institution and produced at the request of examiners or auditors to verify compliance. A financial institution must maintain a Monetary Instrument Log for five years.

**International cash movements.** If you carry or send $10,000 or more in "monetary instruments" into or out of the US, you must submit FinCEN Form 105 (Report of International Transportation of Currency or Monetary Instruments) as you do. A "monetary instrument" includes cash, promissory notes, checks, and money orders without a named payee. This reporting requirement does not cover wire transfers or checks made out to a named payee.

> **What Is and Is Not Cash**
>
> Does the $10K rule apply to the purchase of gold? Yes and
> no. If you want to buy more than $10,000 worth of gold,
> your dealer must report the transaction if you pay by cash
> or cash equivalents, which include cashier's checks and
> money orders. But if you pay by personal check, the dealer
> has no reporting requirement.

**Foreign financial accounts.** If you have an aggregate of $10,000 or
more in foreign financial accounts at any time during the year, you must
file FinCEN Form 114 (Report of Foreign Bank and Financial Accounts,
or FBAR).

In addition, when you file your personal tax return (IRS Form 1040), you
must include Schedule B and check the box asking whether you have a
foreign financial account.

The $10,000 threshold refers to the total of all your foreign financial
accounts. So if on a given day you had $6,000 on deposit with a bank in
Canada and $5,000 in a bank in Mexico, you would need to file an FBAR.

"Foreign financial account" includes a bank account, an account with a
foreign stockbroker or mutual fund, gold held by a foreign custodian, and
a variable annuity or life insurance policy issued by a foreign insurance
company if it has a cash value. Transferring property to a foreign trust
may also trigger a requirement to file an FBAR.

Notably, gold stored in a foreign safe deposit box is not a foreign
financial account.

**Foreign financial assets.** If you have more than $75,000 in specified
foreign financial assets at any time during the year or more than
$50,000 in specified foreign financial assets at the end of the year, you
must report them on IRS Form 8938 (Statement of Foreign Financial
Assets) attached to your personal income tax return. A "specified foreign

financial asset" includes a foreign financial account and, unless held in a custodial account with a U.S. financial institution, (i) foreign issued securities, (ii) any other financial instrument issued or guaranteed by a non-U.S. person, and (iii) any interest in a foreign trust or any 10% or greater interest in a foreign company.

Also notable is that foreign real estate "held directly" — meaning not held through an entity such as a trust, LLC, partnership, or fund — is not reportable. However, rental income from directly held real estate must be reported on IRS Form 1040.

**Foreign limited liability companies.** Assuming that you're using a foreign LLC primarily to hold investments, you almost certainly will be better off having the company elect not to be treated as a foreign corporation. The alternative to corporate status that is available to the LLC depends on whether the company is owned entirely by just one person or by more than one person.

If you are the sole, 100% owner, the LLC can elect to be treated as a disregarded entity by filing IRS Form 8832 (Entity Classification Election). File it no later than 75 days after the company is formed. Then file IRS Form 8858 (Information Return of U.S. Persons with Respect to Foreign Disregarded Entities) every year to report the LLC's activity. Or if your foreign LLC has more than one owner, it should use the same Form 8832 to elect to be treated as a partnership. Then file IRS Form 8865 (Return of U.S. Persons with Respect to Certain Foreign Partnerships) every year to report the LLC's activity.

**Foreign trusts.** Under existing rules, if you transfer money or other property to a foreign trust, you must file IRS Form 3520 (Annual Return to Report Transactions with Foreign Trusts and Receipt of Certain Foreign Gifts) to report the transfer, and IRS Form 3520-A (Annual Information Return of Foreign Trust with a U.S. Owner) to report the income the trust earns on the transferred property and its proceeds. In addition, the type of foreign trust described in this report has been swept into the definition of "foreign financial account," so you must file the FBAR form (to which we refer up above) in connection with the trust. And to give the government a fourth chance to notice that you've set up a foreign trust, you must check the related box in Schedule B when you file your personal tax return.

**Gifts from foreign persons.** Form 3520 is also used to report gifts of money or property received from a foreign person. You must report gifts valued at more than $100,000 from a nonresident alien individual and gifts valued at more than $15,102 (adjusted annually for inflation) from foreign corporations or foreign partnerships. For the purpose of these thresholds, gifts from related parties are aggregated. Form 3520 is an information return, not a tax return, since gifts are not subject to income tax. However, there are significant penalties for failure to file.

**Other reports.** When you file your tax return, you must, of course, include any income or capital gains earned on investments outside the US.

**PFIC Rules.** If the IRS deems an investment a Passive Foreign Investment Company (PFIC), it is taxed at exorbitant rates and carries highly complex reporting rules. Most foreign mutual funds are PFICs, as are certain foreign stocks.

It's not illegal to invest in a PFIC. But practically speaking, the costs of doing it are so onerous that it's not worth it in the vast majority of cases.

If a foreign corporation or investment vehicle meets either of the two conditions below, it will be deemed to be a PFIC.

1) If passive income accounts for 75% or more of gross income, or

2) 50% or more of its assets produce passive income.

The IRS defines passive income as income from interest, dividends, annuities, and certain rents and royalties.

If you own a foreign mutual fund, it probably qualifies as a PFIC. But it's not just foreign mutual funds; it can be any foreign stock that meets either of the above conditions as well.

**PFIC Rules**

Fortunately, there are a couple of ways out, though they aren't ideal.

First, if the PFIC meets certain accounting and reporting requirements, the U.S. investor can elect to treat the PFIC as a Qualified Electing Fund (QEF), which eliminates the punitive tax rates. In practice, you can't count on a PFIC to provide the information needed to make a QEF election. And even if it does, you would be taxed on your share of its income and gains year by year, even if you didn't receive any dividends.

Second, there is, generally speaking, an exemption from PFIC reporting if PFIC holdings do not exceed a certain amount. Check the IRS website for current amounts.

Third, if you hold a PFIC through an IRA or other certain retirement accounts, you may be exempt from Form 8621 PFIC filing requirements.

With the complexity and unfavorable tax rates that come with PFICs, it is usually better to avoid owning them.

(This is not to be construed as tax, investment, or legal advice. As always, discuss your situation with a qualified advisor.)

**Conclusion**

None of these rules prohibits any transaction you might want to undertake. They prohibit undertaking it privately. You're still free to send your money wherever you want and to do so in any way you want. Just don't hurt Uncle Sam's feelings by leaving him out of the loop.

All of the rules cited here are backed up with serious penalties, and most of the penalties can be imposed without a criminal trial. They just take your money — no impartial judge, no jury of your peers, no presumption of innocence. The best way to protect against such a problem is to let your accountant know what you're doing and ask him to prepare the required reports. Being tight-lipped with your accountant is a dangerous practice.

We recommend that you apply the utmost skepticism to any creative plan for making an end run around any of the reporting requirements. People have been arrested for making two $9,000 withdrawals from separate banks within a short period of time. It looked like structuring.

Even if a strategy seems foolproof, before you try it, first talk to an attorney to make sure that it does in fact comply with the law.

Many Americans who've considered internationalizing their affairs are discouraged by the reporting requirements and the stiff penalties that back them up. But that's part of what the rules are for — to keep you and your money in the U.S. and under the government's control. Their second purpose is to give the government the information it will need if it ever decides to compel Americans to repatriate their foreign assets.

The reporting rules discourage Americans from seeking the safety of international diversification. But understanding what the rules are for should encourage you to diversify internationally...while you still can.

## What Internationalization Does *Not* Mean

As you consider the benefits outlined in this report, let's be clear on the one reason **not** to pursue internationalization: to hide assets. If you dream of a numbered account stuffed with a string of zeroes' worth of money secretly earning undeclared income behind Uncle Sam's back... wake up! Those days are gone. Financial privacy is dead, snuffed out by U.S. reporting regulations that blanket the world's financial system.

With the inception of FATCA, the IRS is trying to force every financial institution in the world to report on its American clients. A foreign bank or broker that refuses will effectively be shut out of the U.S. financial system by a punitive withholding tax.

The IRS is succeeding. The U.S. is the world's largest financial services market and, so far, no foreign financial institution has opted to get shut out. To increase the pressure, the U.S. is negotiating tax treaties and cross-border information-sharing agreements with most of the world's governments.

Do not attempt to evade taxes in the name of financial privacy; the penalty for noncompliance is wealth-crushingly severe, and you might face criminal charges as well. We are not fans of the new reporting regime, but comply we must. Do not risk your financial security in a futile attempt to retain financial privacy.

# 13

# RESOURCES

Count yourself lucky if your hometown attorney, accountant, financial planner, bank, or stockbroker is of any use in the matter of going global. Most investors will need to look elsewhere for international financial services and for knowledgeable professional help; they can start with the resources listed here.

## Banking Abroad

Although the number of foreign banks willing to accept Americans is in decline, the following are still open for business with customers from the US.

Each bank below offers an array of account types. Where we indicate "no minimum balance" for an account, that remark may not apply to every type of account you can open with the institution. Also, some banks impose a periodic maintenance fee on small accounts.

Finally, remember that an institution's decisions about opening accounts are made case by case. While there are general guidelines, the bottom line is that the bank or broker always has discretion. Please see Chapter 2 for tips on how to present yourself as a desirable client.

### *Australia*

**Westpac Bank**
Sydney, Australia
Telephone: (+61) 2-9293-9270
To send an email message, use the bank's website at www.westpac.com.au
Account minimum: none
Account opening: remote account opening is welcome, though the account will be restricted until verified. Remote opening is done two

ways:

- Online. To open an account online requires a travel visa number.

- Telephone. Without a visa number, application is submitted over the phone at the number listed above.

An account opened online or over the phone must be verified within the first year. Verification requires an in-person visit with identity documentation. Funds can be transferred into the account once opened. To withdraw funds or make an outbound transfer requires a verified account.

This account opening procedure only applies to Westpac Australia. All Westpac offices outside Australia operate as separately franchised entities.

Westpac is Australia's first and oldest bank, chartered in 1817 as Bank of New South Wales. In 1982, the name was changed to Westpac Banking Corporation following the acquisition of the Commercial Bank of Australia. Westpac offers retail, business, and institutional services. International offices in Singapore, Shanghai, Hong Kong, Beijing, Mumbai, Jakarta, New Zealand, Cook Islands, Fiji, Papua New Guinea, Samoa, Solomon Islands, Tonga, Vanuatu, and London.

## *Austria*

### Valartis Bank
Vienna, Austria
Telephone: (+43) 577-89-100
Email: info@valartis.at
Visit www.valartis.at/en/Home
Account minimum: €150,000
Account opening: does not require an in-person visit to open an account, but a meeting with a bank official must take place within the first year

The bank was established in 1890 as Bankhaus Rosenfeld in the same building in which it resides today. In 2008, it was acquired by the Valartis Group, an international banking and finance organization with offices in Zurich, Geneva, Lugano, Vienna, Liechtenstein, Luxembourg, Singapore, Moscow, and St. Petersburg. The Group's holding company is domiciled in Switzerland. Valartis offers private banking and asset management services and is not a retail bank.

## *Belize*

### Caye Bank
Ambergris Caye, Belize
Telephone: (+501) 226-2388
Contact: Kate Corrigan
Email: kcorrigan@cayebank.bz
Visit www.cayebank.bz
Account minimum: $500
Account opening: does not require an in-person visit

Though Caye Bank does not have a branch in the US, it is experienced with U.S. clients.

Caye Bank is one of the easiest choices for American citizens when it comes to opening a foreign bank account remotely. However, that comes with high fees.

## *Canada*

Each of the Canadian banks below is a full-service, retail institution.

### National Bank of Canada
Montreal, Québec
Offices also in Vancouver, BC, and Toronto
Telephone: 514-394-0296
To send an email message, use the bank's website at www.nbc.ca
Account minimum: none
Account opening: requires in-person visit

Founded in 1859. Services in English, French, and Spanish. Branches in London, Paris, Havana, New York City, Hong Kong, and Pompano Beach and Hollywood, Florida.

## Canadian Imperial Bank of Commerce

Toronto, Ontario
Offices also in Vancouver, BC
Telephone: 416-594-7000
To send an email message, use the bank's website at www.cibc.com
Account minimum: none
Account opening: requires in-person visit; account opening for U.S. clients at the bank's discretion

Organized in 1961 through the merger of The Canadian Bank of Commerce (est. 1867) and the Imperial Bank of Canada (est. 1875).

### *Cook Islands*

## Capital Security Bank

Avarua, Rarotonga
Telephone: +682 22 505
Email: info@csb.co.ck
Visit www.capitalsecuritybank.com
CSB charges an account-opening fee of US$500 and a maintenance fee of US$50 per month.
Account opening: U.S. customers are welcome. No in-person visit is required.

Capital Security Bank (CSB) is an affiliate of Southpac Trust International, the largest licensed trust company in the Cook Islands. CSB is exceptional in three respects. First, it has no links to the US; instead it places money with selected banks in Singapore, Switzerland, Germany, Australia, and New Zealand. Second, it makes loans only against deposits that it is holding and thus has no exposure to loss from bad loans. Third, it maintains an extraordinary level of liquidity — currently with cash equal to 102% of customer deposits.

Accounts are available in all major currencies. Precious metals trading and storage are available through a custodial bank in Lichtenstein.

### *Hong Kong*

**Hang Seng Bank**
Central Hong Kong
83 Des Voeux Road Central
Telephone: (+852) 2822 0228
To contact the bank via email, use the "Contact Us" tab on the homepage,
https://bank.hangseng.com/1/2/home
Account minimum: none
Account opening: in-person visit at a Hong Kong branch required at the
bank's discretion

Hang Seng is a great choice for a Hong Kong bank account. Though it doesn't have any branches in the US, its majority owner is HSBC, which does have branches in the US. The banking products and services offered by Hang Seng and HSBC are nearly identical, though Hang Seng has slightly lower fees.

## *Macau*

**Tai Fung Bank**
Telephone: +853 2832 2323
http://www.taifungbank.com/en_US
Account minimum: none
Account opening: in-person visit at a Macau branch required at the
bank's discretion

Offers China UnionPay credit and debit cards.

## *Jersey*

**Lloyds International**
St. Helier
Telephone: +44 (0) 1539 736626
http://international.lloydsbank.com/
Account minimum: $3,500
Account opening: no in-person visit is required

Lloyds International is a subsidiary of the Lloyds Banking Group, the largest retail bank in the UK. Among other features, it offers checking accounts denominated in pounds sterling, euros, and U.S. dollars.

The bank does work with U.S. citizens, but only if they're living abroad and not a resident in the US.

## *Norway*

### DNB
Oslo
Telephone: (+47) 915 04800
Email: foreign.customers.savings@dnb.no
www.dnb.no/en
Account minimum: €100,000
Account opening: no in-person visit is required

DNB was established in 1822. A series of mergers and acquisitions since 1985 has transformed DNB into Norway's largest financial services group and asset management company. Headquartered in Oslo, the bank has over 500 offices in 23 countries that offer individual, corporate, and institutional services.

## *Singapore*

### UOB
Telephone: (+65) 6222 2121
Email: customer.service@uobgroup.com
Account minimum: S$500 (US$400)
Account opening: in-person visit required

Founded in 1935 as the United Chinese Bank, the name was changed in 1965 to United Overseas Bank. UOB is a leading Asian bank with subsidiaries in Malaysia, Indonesia, Thailand, and China. The UOB Group has a network of 500 offices in 19 countries. UOB is a full-service retail bank.

One product in particular is worth noting: UOB offers unique accounts tied to the gold and silver prices.

### Citibank International Personal Bank Singapore (IPB)
Telephone: (+65) 6224 5757
Account minimum: US$10,000

Account opening: no in-person visit required

IPB is a Singapore subsidiary of Citibank. It's a Singapore company that operates under Singapore law. While it would be optimal to open an account with a purely Singaporean bank like UOB, IPB offers an advantage that no other Singapore bank does as far as we know — the ability to open an account remotely.

An account with IPB is one of the easiest ways to open an offshore bank account in one of the world's best banking jurisdictions. You don't need to travel to Singapore to open this account — it can all be done remotely. You can find the details here:

https://www.ipb.citibank.com.sg/english/forms/english/open-an-IPB-account/form.htm

## *UK*

### Coutts & Co
London
Telephone: (+44) 207-753-1000
Email: international.info@coutts.com
Visit http://international.coutts.com/en/
Account minimum: £5,000
Account opening: requires in-person visit; U.S. clients limited to a UK account; account opening for U.S. clients at the bank's discretion

Coutts & Co is a subsidiary of the Royal Bank of Scotland Group. It offers a range of services, including retail, investment, and private banking and wealth management. Offices or affiliates in Switzerland, Hong Kong, Singapore, UK, Abu Dhabi, Dubai, Qatar, Isle of Man, Channel Islands, and the Cayman Islands.

# International Asset Managers

An international asset manager that offers investment and portfolio planning advice can also assist you in opening a foreign bank account.

- **Weber, Hartmann, Vrijhof & Partners** (WHVP), Zurich

  http://www.whvp.ch/

  Contact: Rob Vrijhof

  Email: info@whvp.ch

  WHVP is suitable for individuals with high net worth who want an elevated level of service. It is a small firm dedicated to developing long-term relationships with its clients, a majority of whom are Americans. It works with Bank Vontobel in Zurich. Minimum account is $500,000.

- **RBC Wealth Management**, Cayman Islands

  http://www.rbcwminternational.com/cayman-anniversary.html

  Contact: Stephen Price

  https://www.rbcwminternational.com/homepage.aspx?directorID=351

  RBC Wealth Management, Cayman Islands is an offshoot of Royal Bank of Canada, but is an independent Caymanian company and falls under Caymanian law, not Canadian law.

## Second Passports and Foreign Residency

### Henley & Partners

A global leader in citizenship planning and citizenship programs.

Visit www.henleyglobal.com.

### Italian Citizenship Assistance Program

Assists people in determining eligibility for and obtaining Italian citizenship through ancestry.

Visit www.icapbridging2worlds.com

## Cayman Islands Immigration Assistance
Assists people in obtaining residency and eventually citizenship in the Cayman Islands.
Nick Joseph
HSM Chambers
Grand Cayman, Cayman Islands
+1 345 815 7425
njoseph@hsmoffice.com
www.hsmoffice.com

## Paraguay Immigration Assistance

Assists people in obtaining Paraguayan permanent residency and citizenship.

Maria Victoria Forero de Reidl
Immigration Manager
Asunción, Paraguay
+595 (0) 21 621 063
vicky@advantageparaguay.com
http://www.advantageparaguay.com/en/

## Andreas Neocleous & Co LLC

If you're serious about obtaining citizenship or residency by making an investment in Cyprus, we recommended that you hire legal counsel to ensure that everything is done correctly. One firm with experience in this area is Andreas Neocleous & Co LLC.

195 Makarios III Avenue
CY-3030 Limassol
PO Box 50613
CY-3608 Limassol
Cyprus
Telephone: +357 25 110000

info@neocleous.com
www.neocleous.com

## St. Kitts & Nevis

If you decide a St. Kitts & Nevis passport is right for you, be sure to only deal with people and firms that have been authorized by the St. Kitts & Nevis government to assist citizenship by investment applicants. A list of authorized persons is available on the St. Kitts & Nevis government's website:

http://www.ciu.gov.kn/?q=node/79

## Belize Immigration Assistance

Assists people in obtaining permanent residency and citizenship in Belize. Can also assist with banking and company formation.

Barrow & Williams
Belize City, Belize
+501 227 5280
attorneys@barrowandwilliams.com
www.barrowandwilliams.com

## Panama Immigration Assistance

Assists people in obtaining permanent residency and citizenship in Panama.

Rainelda Mata-Kelly
Panama City, Panama
+507 216 9299
rmk@mata-kelly.com
www.mata-kelly.com

## Uruguay Immigration Assistance

Assists people in obtaining permanent residency and citizenship in Uruguay.

Fischer & Schickendantz
Montevideo, Uruguay
+598 2915 7468
info@fs.com.uy
www.fs.com.uy

# Gold

## Transport Services

DHL, FedEx, and UPS no longer transport bullion internationally. Two good alternatives are:

## Loomis International

http://www.loomis-international.com/

This company specializes in worldwide, point-to-point secure transportation of valuables.

## Emirates Airlines

http://www.skycargo.com/english/products-and-services/protect/protect-premium/Index.aspx

Based in Dubai, Emirates Airlines offers a transportation service for valuables, with the additional feature of FedEx-style tracking and up-to-the-minute monitoring of your shipment.

# Non-Bank Safe Deposit Boxes

A foreign safe deposit box is the most private arrangement for storing gold. Ideally, your safe deposit box would be in a place you visit for other reasons.

## *Panama*

The country is new to the gold-storage business and the gold market is underdeveloped, though growing rapidly. Panama is easy to reach by air from Atlanta, Dallas, Houston, Miami, Los Angeles, Orlando, and New York City.

Private storage facility:

**Best Safety Boxes**

San Francisco, Calle 50
Building. PH Credicorp Plaza
Ground Floor Local #2
Panama City, Panama
Telephone: (507) 301-0826
Email: info@bestsafetyboxes.com
www.bestsafetyboxes.com

Located in the heart of the banking district. Choose from four box sizes. International wire services available onsite.

## *Austria*

Austria's reputation as a solid jurisdiction for gold storage is centuries old. You can buy and sell gold at just about any bank.

Private storage facility:

**Das Safe**

Auerspergstrasse 1
A-1080 Vienna, Austria
Telephone: (+43) 1-406-6174
Email: info@dassafe.com
www.dassafe.com

Das Safe offers both anonymous and in-name storage. Costs are a bit higher than other options.

## *Dubai*

Dubai has become the financial hub of the Middle East.

Private storage facilities:

## JFT Lockers

Suite 706, Platinum Business Center
Baghdad Street
Al Nahda, Dubai, UAE
Telephone: (+971) 4-257-7427
Email: info@jftlockers.com
www.jftlockers.com

Four box sizes, dual custody, and third-party beneficiary options available.

## *Singapore*

Singapore has one of the most stable, transparent, and corruption-free financial systems in the world. You can buy gold at any bank in the city-state.

Gold purchases are exempt from transaction taxes, provided the gold meets the criteria for "Investment Precious Metals." The types of gold bars and coins (other than Eagles) we discuss in this report would qualify for the exemption.

Private storage facility:

## Certis CISCO

20 Jalan Afifi
Certis CISCO Centre, Singapore 409179
Telephone: (+65) 6747-2888
Email: sales@certissecurity.com
www.certissecurity.com/safedeposit

Part of Certis CISCO Security Group with 50 years of experience in secure valuables storage. Three vault locations in Singapore. Five box sizes.

## *United States*

Private storage facilities:

**Sarasota Vault Depository**

640 South Washington Blvd., #175
Sarasota, FL 34236
Telephone: 941-954-9003
Email contact available through the company's website
www.sarasotavault.com

Temperature-and humidity-controlled facility in hurricane-resistant structure.

**Mountain Vault**

11820 North Cave Creek Rd.
Phoenix, AZ 85020
Telephone: 602-943-9796
Email: information@datamountaininc.com
www.datamountaininc.com/home.html

Vault is embedded in a mountain and fortified with rock, concrete, and steel. Temperature and humidity controlled; backup power system.

## Buying Gold with Custodial Storage

### Perth Mint — Australia

http://www.perthmint.com.au/

A Perth Mint Certificate (PMC) is issued by the Perth Mint in Australia, whose storage facility is widely considered one of the safest in the world.

The gold that a PMC represents can be kept in segregated storage (which the Mint calls "allocated") or in a unique type of pooled storage (which the Mint calls "unallocated"). Such unallocated gold is metal being used in the Mint's manufacturing operations.

For PMC silver, the metal can be kept in segregated ("allocated") storage or in what the Mint calls "pool allocated" storage, which refers to refined silver set aside for customers in the Mint's vaults but without the bars being tagged as belonging to particular customers.

The initial minimum purchase for a PMC is $10,000; for additional purchases, the minimum is $5,000. Unless you're an Australian, you must buy through an approved dealer at the link below.

https://www.perthmint.com/storage/approved-dealers.html

If you want to visit the Mint to pick up your metal, contact your approved dealer. Any approved dealer can also arrange for your metal to be shipped (at your expense) anywhere in the world.

American Eagle gold coins are not available.

### Global Gold — Switzerland

https://www.globalgold.ch/

Global Gold is domiciled in Zug, Switzerland and offers both segregated and pooled gold storage. Metal is vaulted in Zurich, Hong Kong, or Singapore, as you prefer.

Global Gold is one of few custodians/dealers that will accept metal you already own.

You can operate your Global Gold account online and buy and sell whole bars or coins (no fractional trades). Prices are updated on the company's website every 30 seconds.

American Eagle gold coins are available. Global Gold will store metal that you ship to it.

### Silver Bullion — Singapore

https://www.silverbullion.com.sg/Default.aspx

Silver Bullion is a Singapore company that offers a purchase and storage program for precious metals. The company is located inside the Certis CISCO building (see "Foreign safe deposit boxes" above). Account opening and metal purchase and storage can be done at its offices or completed remotely.

All stored metal is fully allocated; metal is not commingled or pooled.

Silver Bullion uses Certis CISCO for its storage of gold that includes full liability protection through a Singapore-based insurance company.

All bullion products are eligible for delivery. The company has zero exposure to any government outside of Singapore.

American Eagle gold coins are not available. Silver Bullion will store metal that you transfer to it.

# Foreign Currencies

### *Foreign currency ETFs*

**CurrencyShares** (http://currencyshares.com/home). Rydex, a prominent innovator in the ETF field, offers nine currency funds, each dedicated to a particular currency (including the five recommended in this report). Each fund's currency is held as demand deposits with JPMorgan Chase Bank, London.

**Wisdom Tree** (http://www.wisdomtree.com/etfs/index-currency.aspx). Brazilian real, Chinese renminbi, and Indian rupee single-currency funds are available. Also offered is a Commodity Currency fund and an Emerging Currency Fund; each holds a basket of currencies. Funds invest in short-term investment-grade instruments. Total return is sought from both money market interest and currency gain against the U.S. dollar.

**ProShares** (http://www.proshares.com/). Euro, Japanese yen, and Australian dollar funds allow both long and short positions as well as 2-to-1 leverage. Funds use currency index futures and index swaps.

# International Stockbrokers

With a foreign broker, you can get direct access to a broader selection of the world's stock exchanges. That means investment choices that aren't available in the U.S. and better execution for the foreign stocks that do trade on a U.S. exchange.

A foreign brokerage, unlike a foreign bank account, is generally much easier to open remotely than a foreign bank account. This is because a foreign brokerage account offers fewer features than a bank account. Establishing a foreign brokerage account could be a relatively easy way for you to establish a foreign financial account without having to travel.

## OCBC - Singapore

http://www.iocbc.com/

OCBC Securities is the brokerage affiliate of OCBC Bank. Its online trading division, iOCBC, executes trades in stocks, futures, and foreign currencies and options. Although the range of products is limited, the list of exchanges you can reach with an iOCBC account is impressive:

- United States: NYSE, AMEX, NASDAQ

- UK: London Stock Exchange

- Australia: Australian Stock Exchange

- China: Shanghai Stock Exchange, Shenzhen Stock Exchange; B-shares only. ("B-shares" are shares in companies based in mainland China that trade on either the Shanghai or Shenzhen stocks exchanges and eligible for foreign investment.) B-shares trade on the Shanghai exchange in U.S. dollars and on the Shenzhen exchange in Hong Kong dollars.

- Hong Kong: Hong Kong Stock Exchange

- Japan: Tokyo Stock Exchange

- Indonesia: Indonesia Stock Exchange

- Malaysia: Bursa Malaysia

- Philippines: Philippine Stock Exchange

- Singapore: Singapore Exchange

- Thailand: Stock Exchange of Thailand

Complete mobile trading from a smartphone is available. Consult the website for details.

Minimum to open an account is $2,000.

Nationality restrictions: U.S. citizens and residents can open an account but are barred from trading on U.S. exchanges. Thus iOCBC would be a good choice for an American only if you want to trade in Asian markets.

iOCBC will open accounts remotely.

## Monex Boom Securities - Hong Kong

https://baby.boom.com.hk/en/index.asp

Monex Boom Securities is part of the Monex Group, one of Japan's largest online brokers. It is an online broker that trades only in the following markets:

- United States: NYSE, NASDAQ

- Australia: Australia Stock Exchange

- China: Shanghai Stock Exchange, Shenzhen Stock Exchange; B- and H-shares. ("H-shares" are shares of companies incorporated in mainland China that trade on the Hong Kong Stock Exchange in Hong Kong dollars.)

- Hong Kong: Hong Kong Stock Exchange

- Japan: Tokyo, Fukuoka, Nagoya, Osaka, and Sapporo stock exchanges

- Indonesia: Indonesia Stock Exchange

- Malaysia: Bursa Malaysia

- Philippines: Philippine Stock Exchange

- Singapore: Singapore Exchange

- South Korea: Korea Exchange

- Taiwan: Taiwan Stock Exchange

- Thailand: Stock Exchange of Thailand

You can hold cash in a Boom account in your choice of six currencies: Hong Kong dollar, Chinese renminbi, U.S. dollar, Japanese yen, Singapore dollar, and Australian dollar.

Commissions are competitive with other online brokers. Monex Boom does charge something we haven't come across anywhere else — a small fee for processing dividend income. There is an account-opening fee of HK$200 (≈US$25) and a yearly administrative fee of HK$200 as well. There is no account minimum.

Nationality restrictions: U.S. citizens/residents accepted as clients but barred from trading on U.S. exchanges.

Monex Boom Securities will open accounts remotely.

**Panama Wall Street – Panama**

https://panamawallstreet.com/

Panama Wall Street is an online broker and is the largest brokerage firm in Panama. It executes trades in stocks, options, futures, and foreign currencies. Exchanges you can reach through an account include:

- United States: NYSE, NASDAQ, AMEX

- Canada: Toronto Stock Exchange

- Australia: Australian Stock Exchange

- Austria: Vienna Stock Exchange

- Germany: Frankfurt Stock Exchange

- Italy: Borsa Italiana

- Netherlands: Euronext Amsterdam

- Norway: Oslo Stock Exchange

- Poland: Warsaw Stock Exchange

- Sweden: NASDAQ OMX Nordic Exchange

- Spain: Bolsa de Madrid

- Switzerland: Swiss Exchange

- UK: London Stock Exchange

- Hong Kong: Hong Kong Stock Exchange

Customer support is provided in both English and Spanish.

Minimum to open an account is $5,000.

Nationality restrictions: None.

Panama Wall Street will open accounts remotely.

## OneTRADEx — Cayman Islands

http://onetradex.com/

OneTRADEx is a discount broker with an online trading platform with access to markets in 23 countries.

You can also trade the following with your account: options, futures, forex, bonds, ETFs, CFDs, and commodities, including physical gold.

OneTRADEx accepts U.S. clients - but only if they are not U.S. residents - and will open accounts remotely.

## Living Abroad

If you're looking to be part of a community of like-minded souls, browse the Fellowship for Intentional Community directory of communities (http://www.ic.org/directory/map/) to investigate intentional communities located just about anywhere in the world.

Naturally, we're partial to Doug Casey's La Estancia de Cafayate (http://www.laest.com/), a 550-hectare (1360 acre) secluded wine and residential sporting estate.

## Freedom for Your IRA

For help in forming a self-directed IRA, inquire with:

- **The Entrust Group** (http://www.theentrustgroup.com/) Provider and administrator of self-directed IRAs.

- **Sovereign International Pension Services** (http://www. sovereignpensionservices.com/) Sovereign International Pension Services is an independent IRA administrator for self-directed plans.

- **GoldStar Trust** (http://www.goldstartrust.com/) This custodian can handle unconventional, self-directed IRAs invested in precious metals, annuities, or an LLC.

## Foreign Limited Liability Companies

The premier jurisdictions for foreign LLCs are Nevis (in the Caribbean) and the Cook Islands (in the South Pacific, northeast of New Zealand). We prefer the Cook Islands, because it isn't dependent on the U.S. for airline connections, banking, or anything else. And — at least for Americans in the Western states — the Cook Islands is easier to reach than Nevis.

The Southpac Group (http://www.southpactrust.com/), headquartered in the Cook Islands, provides trust and company management services in both jurisdictions.

## International Trusts

To learn about a cost-conscious international trust program (the only one we know of), contact:

- Passport Financial (http://passporttrustinfo.com/downloads/passport-trust-kit-download/)

Two attorneys who specialize in using international trusts and LLCs are:

Robert B. Martin, Jr.
Escondido, CA
Mobile: 626-840-3472
Telephone: 760-670-3735
Email: rbmartin@rbmartinlaw.com
Website: www.rbmartinlaw.com

Michael Chatzky
Chatzky and Associates
San Diego, CA
Telephone: 858-457-1000
Email: mgchatzky@aol.com

## Tax Filing Preparation and Compliance

David L. Hillary, Jr., CPA
Phone: +1 317-222-1803
david@intaxact.com
http://intaxact.com/

Piascik Certified Public Accountants
4470 Cox Road, Suite 250
Glen Allen, Virginia 23060
Phone: +1 (866) 501-4013

info@piascik.com
http://www.piascik.com/our-expertise/practice-specialties/
international-tax

## Other Internationalization Sources

We also recommend our affiliated, free publication, the *International Man Communiqué*. You can subscribe by visiting:

www.InternationalMan.com

*Crisis Investing* is a unique service that will uncover the deep-value "blood in the streets" investment opportunities waiting behind the news that frightens others away. Internationalize your portfolio with fundamentally sound businesses whose stock prices have been hammered down by fear, crisis, and politically caused distortions. Learn more here:

https://www.caseyresearch.com/products/crisis-investing

There is no guarantee for how long any of the above institutions will continue to welcome American clients. If you're an American citizen, it's better to open an account sooner than later. This is a list of services that are available for international diversification at the time of publishing. It does not constitute an endorsement. Each reader should continually evaluate the appropriateness of a service for his/her needs.

# 14

# CONCLUSION

We hope we've given you a sense of how broad your options are for internationalization.

If you're new to the world of globalizing your wealth and possibly yourself, the choices can seem a bit too broad. But don't let the size of the menu prevent you from making a few smart choices.

There is much that you can do. And now you may be asking yourself a simple question:

If I go global, will I be a target? If I diversify myself and my assets outside of the United States, will I receive unnecessary scrutiny from the government?

Our answer? Absolutely. Yes, you're going to be a target.

But guess what — so is everyone else. All the people who stick their heads in the sand and fail to prepare will also be targets. The government is desperate for cash. So are some of your neighbors. From here on, anyone with assets is a target, with a bright red bullseye painted on his wallet.

You are going to be a target of those in the sinking ship no matter what you do. You have a choice, though: You can be a target and protect yourself by internationalizing your assets through all the legal means available, or you can do nothing and be a target that's easy to hit.

All those reporting requirements sure look daunting. Are all the extra forms worth the hassle? It certainly seems like an awful paperwork burden, doesn't it? Maybe so. But consider this: given the direction the U.S. is taking, do you think your taxes are going to become more complicated or less complicated?

You're going to be filling out reams of new tax paperwork each year no matter what you do. Here the choice is black or white. Fill out forms and be protected, or fill out forms and stay exposed.

Going global is your ultimate protection in uncertain times — it wins you the freedom to move about this world, secure in the knowledge that you and your family will remain healthy, wealthy, and safe no matter how fast things start tumbling downhill.

Gaining that protection takes some effort, but you were probably motivated before you began reading this report. And if we've done our job in explaining how dangerous it is to keep all your eggs in one basket, you're now even more motivated. Perhaps you can see that time is running short.

## What's Your Next Step?

Do something. Get your assets moving in the right direction, and soon. Start evaluating the opportunities to internationalize any aspect of your life. There are many steps — such as moving your brokerage account offshore — that you can take without even leaving your living room.

Approach internationalization as you would plan a trip to a distant corner of the world. The language, culture, and customs of an unfamiliar land require some getting used to. But not long after arriving, the unfamiliar starts to become the routine. Taking your assets on an international journey will bring you the same experience. It's a learning experience.

## About the Contributors

**Doug Casey** is chairman of Casey Research. A highly respected author, publisher, speaker, and professional investor, he literally wrote the book on internationalization and crisis investing. His book *Crisis Investing* hit #1 on the *New York Times* Best Sellers list, and his 1978 book *The International Man* is the original handbook on internationalizing your finances and your life. Doug is a sought-after speaker who has appeared on hundreds of radio and TV shows. He divides his time between homes in Colorado, New Zealand, and Argentina.

**Nick Giambruno** is Doug Casey's globetrotting companion and the Senior Editor of *International Man*. He writes about economics, offshore banking, second passports, surviving a financial collapse, foreign trusts and companies, geopolitics, and value investing in crisis markets, among other topics. He is also the Senior Editor of the *Crisis Investing* investment publication. In short, Nick's work helps people make the most of their personal freedom and financial opportunity around the world. He's lived in Europe and worked in the Middle East, most recently in Beirut and Dubai, where he covered regional banks and other companies for an investment house. Nick is a CFA charterholder and holds a bachelor's degree in finance, *summa cum laude*.

## About the Publisher

Founded by Doug Casey, Casey Research has been helping self-directed investors earn superior returns through innovative investment research designed to take advantage of market dislocations.

Casey Research publishes a number of subscription newsletters. Find out more at:

www.CaseyResearch.com